HELL FOR LEATHER

Also by Marcus Armytage

GENEROUS

Hell for Leather
A CHAMPION'S DIARY
RICHARD DUNWOODY
with MARCUS ARMYTAGE

PARTRIDGE PRESS

LONDON · NEW YORK · TORONTO · SYDNEY · AUCKLAND

TRANSWORLD PUBLISHERS LTD
61–63 Uxbridge Road, London W5 5SA

TRANSWORLD PUBLISHERS (AUSTRALIA) PTY LTD
15–25 Helles Avenue, Moorebank, NSW 2170

TRANSWORLD PUBLISHERS (NZ) LTD
3 William Pickering Drive,
Albany, Auckland

Published 1993 by Partridge Press
a division of Transworld Publishers Ltd
Copyright © Richard Dunwoody and Marcus Armytage 1993

A catalogue record for this book is available from the British Library.

ISBN 185225 2227

Typeset in 11/13pt Century Old Style by
Chippendale Type Ltd, Otley, West Yorkshire.
Printed in Great Britain by
Mackays of Chatham, Chatham, Kent.

For Carol, George, Gillian, Roddy and Sue

ACKNOWLEDGEMENTS

Our thanks to George and Gillian Dunwoody, Brough Scott and the staff at the *Racing Post*.

HELL FOR LEATHER

INTRODUCTION

OUTSIDE, RAIN DRIFTING HORIZONTALLY down from the Ridgeway pummels the window panes of Hyperion House and rattles the door. It's dark, very dark. In the kitchen the dog growls at the prowling wind. Off the Downs, chalky torrents turn puddles into ponds, gateways into quagmires, while drains, unable to cope, gush like river sources. It's one of those mornings – no matter the amount of waterproofing, how waxed the coat, how thick the gloves, how tight the collar to the neck – you're in for a soaking, rainwater marination. You know the feeling. Leaks appear first at the collar and cuffs; the wet, defying gravity, is absorbed up the sleeves like rising damp in the walls of an old house, and down the neck like ink into blotting paper. On mornings like this, Zafonic, a horse that in a day can earn what chasers might win in a lifetime, would have stayed in bed.

This is the jumping game though. It's midwinter. No-one's really in it for the money. Sure, a few successful trainers make a good living, a few of the top jockeys, maybe a lucky owner – but even if you're given a horse it costs £10,000 a year to keep it in training and, for most, there are precious few occasions to win that back.

Unsung heroes – the headlads – have no chance. Clifford Baker at Jackdaw's Castle or Corky Brown at Seven Barrows, up before the sparrows and on the feeding round. Headlads spend a lifetime in the job until put out to grass by crippling arthritis or old age. There's the occasional punt at good odds if their old mates get their information right, but they are never courted by Allied Dunbar salesmen with complicated index-linked pension plans. They earn little above a modest wage other than a small percentage of a small percentage of the prize-money. Good days they'll back winners; bad days and the bookmakers are only too glad to relieve their already light pockets. What chance have they got?

Jockeys? You wonder sometimes what motivates them, it's a peculiar, unique way of life, that of a jump jockey. I dare say they are no more competitive than any other athletes, but there is something different about combining with half a ton of horseflesh, getting it right together, forming a bond with an animal as strong as that between shepherd and sheepdog, poacher and lurcher, with mutual respect and admiration for each other. You curse them at times, you don't understand them at other times, they bite you, they kick you and they fall on you. Yet, combine as a team, bring the sheep off the hill, catch the rabbit by lamp, ride a winner and there's no better feeling, no greater thrill.

A jockey will go to the end of the earth to satisfy an addiction to win. And the more you win the stronger the compulsion, the greater the addiction. It's powerful stuff, just takes a couple of sniffs, adrenalin junkeys hopelessly hooked like the drug addicts down Piccadilly on a Saturday night. But jump racing is not at home to complacency, confidence yes, but not smug complacency. Ride the winner of the Tote Gold Cup and you might find that an hour later Dr Rooker is waving you goodbye on your way to Cheltenham General, strapped to a scoop-stretcher in the back of an ambulance breathing a cocktail of anaesthetizing gas and oxygen. It's hardly champagne and orange or gin and tonic. You'd think it was a fable, a parable, only it's a true story.

But to be the best requires a dedication, strength of character and a temperament beyond a natural talent. It probably makes you bloody awkward to live with. You've got to have that bit more killer instinct than the rest. You've got to be prepared on occasions to walk over 'friends'. And there has to be more calculating bastard in you than the guy who is runner-up. Plenty have had a natural talent – and how their colleagues have envied the silken hands, eye for a stride, ability to get a horse jumping and running – only for it to be wasted because they haven't had the tunnel vision, the burning ambition, the drive, that contract-killer's zeal for his job. They just turned over and switched the alarm off, pulled the duvet over their careers and rang the trainer to say they'd had a puncture.

There's the temptation to think the top jockeys are mercenaries, talented enough to make quick and good money, treating horses as a means to an end, printing presses for the Royal Mint. Get in, get out. As quick as possible, as intact as possible, for as much as possible. Sure, the Scudamores, Dunwoodys, Dwyers, Doughtys, Nivens feather their nests when they can, set themselves up for retirement and perhaps a rainy day. They don't want to rush into a new job when it's all over. But this is no brief skirmish, this war will be waged over about fifteen years. And the greater chance when you jack in the A levels, pluck up the courage to break the bad news to the careers officer at school is that, apart from him laughing, you'll never make it to the top half dozen. How many would-be Nigel Mansells have got no further than banger racing? How many Faldos no further than the 19th hole?

The most talented have tended to make their own luck, have been offered the best jobs at a lesser talent's expense or to replace a retiring talent, but even Peter Scudamore, Richard Dunwoody, Lester Piggott and Pat Eddery still needed, still need something more than a platonic relationship with Lady Luck.

We're going to be taking you to Cheltenham and Aintree, the power and the glory. Groupies hanging around the weighing-room steps, air-punching victory salutes, fat pay cheques from Weatherbys – you bet it isn't. More like a roller-coaster ride which comes off its rails. You're at Hexham in the snow, the only female hanging around you is the persistent old dear dressed in a St John Ambulance uniform, only after that fall, you see three of her. The punch is one of despair, it's into the turf only it hurts you more than it hurts the ground, and the pay cheque is signed by a trustee of the Injured Jockeys Fund.

A jockey's hours are long, often anti-social, more often than not unglamorous, like laddered tights or sweaty jockstraps. We see the pink frock on top or the smartly dressed jockey in the parade ring, we read about it in the papers, watch it on television; we don't get to see the dirty underwear or the supermodel's dandruff. It's like reading James Herriot and thinking what fun to live the life of a vet, great fun, indeed, until the first cow pats you on the head.

Jockeys can't do a lot of things. They can't go and watch a soccer match on a Saturday afternoon, can't go out to dinner on a Friday or to the flicks midweek. For ten months a year they can't indulge in cream buns or ice-cream and no second helpings of turkey on Christmas Day. Small things like that. Well, they can but it's difficult, and it's often better not to be seen drinking in racecourse bars these days, it's verging on the unprofessional that is. It is all so professional now, no longer can the champion jockey be the laughing cavalier. No longer is it acceptable to be kidnapped in your own car because the missus kicked you out of your hotel room – you slept under a blanket in the car, and some Scouser knicked the car – all two nights before the Grand National. No, now the onus, for better or for worse, is on total dedication, professionalism, surgical analysis, po-faces win or lose. What sport isn't? Colin Jackson doesn't train over hurdles on which are precariously balanced glasses of champagne. David Gower's lark in a fast car or light plane is no longer an acceptable substitute for an hour-long batting session in the nets. Racing's become a little like that. The mathematical equation, the end result of which is business with a capital B, no longer includes fun.

Outside Hyperion House it's still raining. Inside, Richard Dunwoody, one of racing's oft-sung heroes, worshipped in the aisles of the chapels of St Ladbrokes, wakes. The alarm bells of his mental timer beat his electric clock by a couple of minutes and he switches it off to prevent it disturbing his wife, Carol. It is ten minutes before six in the morning, an often anti-social start to another day at the office. He'd like to pull the duvet over his head but does not give it a thought. He is used to the routine: bathroom; clothes on; kettle on; step into a pair of patiently waiting, highly polished brown boots. David Nicholson, his trainer, is a stickler for military tidiness, no buff when it could be shined, no dull reflection when the brass buckle should twinkle. He packs a change of clothes, grabs the recharged mobile phone, gulps down a cup of tea and legs it to the car, lit up by the security light. The engine purrs into life, windscreen wipers whip into action, the car splashes out the drive and on its way to Jackdaw's Castle in Gloucestershire.

He'd be hungry if he had time to think about it. His is a career of self-denial which goes beyond giving the sweet trolley a miss in the Peking Dynasty on a Saturday night. The physical aches and pains, usually borne in silence to all but the physiotherapist, are evident in rainbow-coloured bruising. A pathologist would tell you how he had met his grisly end if he could see some of the bruises. Like Stiltons, each a different shade of colour depending on maturity. The fresh green one at the base of the spine, the yellowing around a collar-bone, the tight swelling around a knee joint, all as dark and evil as it is outside this wet morning.

There are the mental aches and pains too for the perfectionist's perfectionist. You'd like to get it through to him that perfection is not always attainable when your partner is a horse. It isn't like Torvill and Dean, there's no *Bolero* in the background when you ride a race, you can't tell Torvill she's doing it all wrong. So, with only one in ten winners, is Dunwoody truly satisfied with his own performance. And Scudamore, the reigning champion, is snapping at his heels in the championship. Richard keeps saying he wants to get Cheltenham and Liverpool out of the way before he lets the pressure of championships and numerical games get to him, when a selling plate is worth the same score as the Whitbread Gold Cup. The pressure's getting through all right.

But what does this cold, wet, late January sweaty jockstrap of a day hold in store for our would-be champion? A 45-minute drive into Gloucestershire; a session schooling horses at Nicholson's new yard, Jackdaw's Castle; a piece of toast; another cup of coffee, taken on the hoof. Both toast and coffee send their most sincere apologies for breakfast. A change into something dry, from boxers outwards, and on to the races if it passes the weather inspection. A sit in the sauna. Five rides at this season's strike rate – that's the probability of a winner, the possibility of a faller, and home again. Supper on the table for 8.30 to coincide with homework, the evening screening of the day's highlights on SIS. That's not the all of it either.

He has to book his rides for tomorrow and the day after; book a flight to Ireland for a couple of rides on Sunday. 'You're glad when you get a spell of freezing weather and racing's off for a week,' he says. 'I'll be at my lowest ebb at the height of the season, jaded just when I need to be at my best. After that it gets easier, days off when we get to May, a chance to recharge the batteries.' His threequarters of an hour in the sauna – from which he'll exit, towel draped about the empty waist, feeling something like a human raisin, speaking quietly, his mouth as lubricated as a dried flower display – is spent going through possible rides, studying five-day entries, possible runners, deciding on probable winners, trying to avoid the possible fallers.

Two paragraphs for this lifetime in the day of Richard Dunwoody? No way. Five minutes up the road he pulls into the Prince of Wales at Challow Station where he meets colleague Carl Llewellyn, who won the 1992 Grand National on Party Politics. Thursdays, regardless of weather, are schooling days and besides the yard's own understudies, Nicholson likes to employ another experienced, senior jockey to help out with the schooling – home practice at jumping for horses. They share the lift and their company on the way. Richard drives.

The conversation is stilted at this time of day. Stanford-in-the-Vale, Faringdon, Burford, Stow-on-the-Wold. In the summer it's a route through rural England into the Cotswolds, drystone walls, a striking picture-postcard landscape, cow parsley and purple wisteria. It conjures up images of fox cubs playing, picnics in long grass, over-weight American tourists eating ice-cream and long queues behind caravans. In January the fox on the side of the road is run over, a wet ignominious grave. A placard advertises 'Kev's hotdogs' in a lay-by. Kev hasn't arrived yet, but you can imagine the smell of those fried onions – like tear gas. The Americans are in Florida and the muddy spray from the car in front smudges the windscreen.

Turn off the Tewkesbury Road to the right, first left through a five-bar farmgate which requests in no uncertain terms that it be kept shut, wiggle down an unassuming stone track and suddenly, out of the dark, Jackdaw's Castle dazzles you, a spaceship just landed, bright lights, emissions of steam from a chimney. It is built in the crater left by old quarry working, consequently all but the clock tower are out of sight until you swing into the ante-yard, a Cotswold version of Brookside meets Emmerdale Farm. New stone houses, bungalows, office buildings and eighty stables, the quarry community. At the moment, before the Virginia creeper and ivy has broken the sharp lines and symmetricality of the newly built, it appears more practical than beautiful. It will be, mind you, when the new-cut stone is weathered, the scars of digger and bulldozer are healed, the shelterbelts, at present a sea of waving plastic tubes, are grown. Aesthetes will have to wait.

'Mornin', Woody.' He is greeted in the tackroom as lads and lasses dig out their waterproofs from their respective lockers, tie snotty handkerchiefs round their necks as a last resort, and pick up waterproof sheets for the horses. Some, resigned, or hopeful of respite, don't bother, they accept they will get wet, they're used to it. Richard glances at the list pairing lads to horses, picks up his saddle, is handed a bridle and sets off to tack up his mount.

The schooling goes well. It is an important part of training chasers and hurdlers. First you get them jumping well, enjoying it, and then you speed it up so that when they meet a fence at 30 mph on a racecourse for the first time they don't forget to take-off. A bit like an actor rehearsing his lines, and the jockey hopes he won't have to do too much prompting. It happens sometimes though, horses not taking off at a fence or finding their nerve has deserted them at the last minute. Usually, those are the bad falls unless you're thrown clear – but that's when the horse does a handstand, you do an impersonation of Jesus on the cross trying to keep some semblance of balance, and then thump, no time to roll, just thump into the ground like a wooden post hit by a sledgehammer.

So a successful schooling session is a satisfying part of the job, rain or no rain. You learn more about a horse than you would in a canter or a gallop. It tells you something about his intelligence, his willingness to learn, his agility, his courage. Some are naturals, others are slow learners, some never quite get the hang of it, some try with the best intentions, others need their hands held. Nicholson, a former jockey himself, points and bawls instructions. He may have the finest jockey in the country riding for him but he's very much the employer. His jockey is the employee: to do as he's told and rollocked when he doesn't. On the whole it is a good relationship, moulded by seven winters, cemented by success. Racing needs its strong characters like The Duke, a nickname acquired from his days as an apprentice.

So the slice of toast is taken on the hoof. A brief chat with Nicholson about runners later that week, a brief reflection on the morning's schooling. Was Richard happy with so and so? Would another horse be suitable for the stable amateur at Warwick next weekend? Back, Stow-on-the-Wold, Burford, Faringdon, Stanford-in-the-Vale, at the Prince of Wales he drops Carl off. Richard is back home by 9.45 a.m. His lightest weight at Taunton today is 10st 6lb. It does not require a sauna so he'll read the newspapers in a hot bath for threequarters of an hour, a rover-phone at his side, form book and towel on the bathroom floor. You can lose a couple of pounds in a hot bath and it's less suffocating than a sauna. He'll make his second call of the day to Robert Kington, his agent who books him rides. Of those rides which he's offered, Robert, a former jockey, advises what to accept and what to reject. Of those he's not offered, he advises what and what not to ring up for. He's a permanent contact point for Richard. The two of them together can cast a wider net ensuring few winners slip through. It's part of the competitiveness of it all. Two similar jockeys and the difference between the pair will be their agents.

Taunton's first race is at 1.30 p.m., so Richard will leave home at 11 a.m. Punctually. He's the punctual, meticulous type, a trait inherited from his mother. He picks up colleague Simon McNeill on the way. If every sport has a genuine nice-guy then Simon is jump racing's. It is an awful word 'nice' but Simon has too much of it to have ever been a champion. He's great company, steady as a rock in a sometimes perilous sea, a good mucker of the Dunwoodys. If he was a racehorse he'd be described as workmanlike. He was a late developer and just when he got to the age when most of his colleagues start thinking about retirement, he started having some success by winning the Queen Mother Champion Chase on Katabatic. No-one, not one person, begrudges him that success and that alone in this often cut-throat sport is something of an achievement.

Richard will see action in five of the seven races. Taunton is a fast, sharp track, very tight bends and a trappy third-last fence, which is catching out horses this season. It is, in racing parlance, considered something of a gaff (second-rate) track. In the summer it's a living nightmare to ride. Horses invariably go split-arse and slip on lush grass round its two very sharp bends. If you've been to a grade-one track the day before, this is like Indy car racing after Silverstone. But on the soft it is better and jockeys are more sensible.

In the opener, the Pickeridge Novices' Claiming Hurdle for four-year-olds over two miles and three furlongs, Peter Scudamore's mount beats Richard's Eau d'Espoir by two lengths. As runner-up he picks up 5 per cent of £454 on top of his £73.70 riding fee. 'She ran well,' comments Richard. 'Scu was on the hot favourite. My horse has been prone to making mistakes but ran up to her best.' Those comments will be assimilated into the Dunwoody mental computer. His race descriptions are to the point, factual and without emotion. The observations of anything that doesn't matter don't come into it. Just the stark facts, how it jumped, how it's best ridden, the ground, trip, breathing. When I do this once a week each ride's an adventure, a chapter in a book, a story in itself, I notice little things beyond the 'chsd ldrs, hdwy 6th, led and mistake 2 out, kept on but hdd near fin; Ran to best' which is recorded in Superform Weekly. Twenty rides a week and it all becomes very matter-of-fact.

Half an hour later Richard is a mudsplattered second, again, on Bill Turner's The Slater in the two mile three furlong Bickenhall Novices' Handicap Chase. That's when the frustration begins to creep in despite being beaten a comfortable twelve lengths by Dubacilla. 'He made very bad mistakes at the fourth last and second last. He travelled well until then. He was still in touch with a chance when he galloped into the second last. Lucky to stand up. The winner might turn out to be quite good.' The winner does turn out to be quite good. And modesty forbids: for 'Lucky to stand up' read, 'Well sat.'

Another half-hour. It is still raining, mottled grey clouds hurry across the Somerset sky. Beading sweat prevents the mud specks congealing on Richard's now mottled grey face. Little time to think. A quick look at the racecard to check the next is the two-mile hurdle. John Buckingham, Richard's valet, has put out the colours for Ron Hodges' Tiger Claw. The race is won by Scu who has now ridden a double. More frustration. Martin Pipe, reigning champion trainer, and Scu, reigning champion jockey, on a roll. The championship is all beginning to look so inevitable now. Tiger Claw falls at the last, the mission on this occasion not nearly accomplished. It had not been to win, well win if you can, but Tiger Claw was out of the handicap, and therefore running at a weight disadvantage. This season he had lost his form. 'I was in fifth place riding for fourth,' says Richard. 'Saving something for the run in. Just didn't get his landing gear out.' A couple of bruises, that's all, like a rabbit that gets a good shaking from a dog and escapes. Sore for a couple of days. From five rides this was the possibility.

Things are going from moderate to bad by Dunwoody standards. He watches the next on the closed-circuit television in the changing room. Scu gets the treble up on Riverside Boy. 'Brilliant on it,' he says. 'Shouldn't have won but Scu got it home. Pipe's horses are beginning to run very well.' Richard's mount in the next, the EBF Novices' Hurdle, is the favourite Tudor Fable, having his first run over obstacles. He disappoints. He is owned by Tim Collins who also owns Remittance Man. Expectations are high though it is amazing how rarely lightning strikes twice. Remittance Men are once in a lifetime and poor Tudor Fable has a hard act to follow. When he returns to the changing room Richard hears that Scu has been banned for four days for excessive use of the whip on Riverside Boy in the previous race. 'I'd be lying if I said I wasn't in some way relieved,' he says. It will give him a breather in the championship. At the same time he, like Scu, is frustrated about the rules that govern the use of the whip. Scu would not have won without it and for the 1993/94 season they will be twice as stringent again. The whole thing's a muddle. The integrity of the sport relies upon jockeys trying to win, and yet try too hard and you're penalized. We'd just got used to the ten-hit rule, it has worked well of late, and now we have to start again.

The last race provides further relief when he rides Grouseman to win the Levy Board Handicap Hurdle for Henrietta Knight. 'Mark Richards who had ridden him before told me he would run well. He never travelled at all. The track was a bit sharp and even jumping the second last I never thought I'd win.' The post-race comments become more animated after a victory. He wants to continue pointing out the more crucial, pivotal moments. 'I switched him to the stands rail,' he says suggestively – that was the split-second decision that won it. 'He started to run on a bit going to the last and when I'd given him a couple of reminders he flew and won quite easily by a length.' From five rides that was the probability.

Showered and changed, he's out of the course by 6 p.m. and back home by 7.30. How he wishes he could be spirited there. There will still be phone calls to make, trainers to talk to, things to organize, weight to be lost for tomorrow but supper to be eaten. He's too tired to watch the SIS recording of the day's sport, it is after all still a sport. He's driven 240 miles, ridden twelve miles. Statistically the probable and possible both occurred, a winner and a faller. But that victory in the last brought a smile to Dunwoody's features. The grin reveals a missing tooth, not lost in an argument with a horse's hoof but in a playground accident at school. The winner was one of those one-in-tens, a satisfactory end to the day. You'll get face-ache if you do too much smiling Richard. Brushing through the birchwood switches, cramming at the open ditches, this is life in the fast lane, this is split-arse, split-second stuff, this is hell for leather.

CHAPTER ONE

THE EARLY YEARS

IN ORDER TO UNDERSTAND why a thoroughbred runs fast, or when the racehorse is a yearling or foal, to help predict how fast that horse will run over what distance, experts look at the pedigree. Though conformation clearly plays its part, a thoroughbred's price tag will, to a lesser or greater degree, depend upon its pedigree. Breeding has never followed hard-and-fast rules. Red Rum was not bred to win three Grand Nationals for example. The resultant offspring of a Derby winner and an Oaks winner might be handsomely bred, strikingly good looking, but in reality it might not be capable of winning an egg-and-spoon race. The son of a Derby runner-up and Oaks second might result in a Derby winner as it did with Commander in Chief in 1993. On the other hand an expert can look through the pedigree of the year's 2,000 Guineas winner and point out which attributes – the stamina, the speed, the flowing movement – come from which side of the family. The same can be said of us to some extent. It can have been of little surprise to the great Baroque composer Johann Sebastian

Bach, for example, that between the cantatas and sonatas, two of his sons, Carl Philipp Emanuel and Johann Christian, should both become well-known classical composers themselves. A combination of breeding and being spoonfed music during their formative years – it's the Mozart's-old-man-was-a-violinist syndrome.

Likewise Peter Scudamore, eight times champion jump jockey, Richard Dunwoody's predecessor as champion and Martin Pipe's first jockey, was the son of Michael Scudamore who won the Gold Cup on Linwell in 1957 and the Grand National on Oxo two years later. His great-grandfather John Scudamore, while not involved in racing, was nevertheless a renowned horseman. Again, a combination of breeding and being brought up in an atmosphere of horsetalk and pony rides. Richard Dunwoody is a natural horseman. We cannot begin to quantify how much of this is breeding, though I'm sure it comes into play, or how the environment in which he was brought up influenced the shape of his career. However, a glance at both should give us some idea.

Richard's father, George Dunwoody, was born in 1919 and was a successful amateur rider and trainer in Ireland. He rode over 100 winners and retired shortly after riding Flashing, a horse he trained himself, to win at Down Royal on 12 May 1969, his fiftieth birthday. It was George who introduced racing to the Dunwoody side of the family. His father, Richard's grandfather, Thomas Rutherford Dunwoody, had been a bank manager and farmer in Monaghan, just south of the border between Northern Ireland and Eire, not far from Armagh. Thomas used to go racing with friends who owned horses but frowned upon George's eagerness to pursue a career with these animals. However he'd given George a good pony, which had fired up his enthusiasm for riding across country, be it hunting or racing. On leaving school, against his father's better judgement, George joined the trainer Cecil Brabazon, who trained on the Curragh, as his pupil-assistant. George is not a very tall man but it was assumed he would grow too heavy to make a living as a professional jockey, so he remained amateur, unpaid. At the time Aubrey Brabazon, Cecil's son (who later rode Cottage Rake to win the Gold Cup three years in succession for Vincent O'Brien beginning in 1948 and was one of the great post-war Irish jockeys), was a young apprentice on the flat for another local trainer, Darby Rogers.

'I was at the Curragh for four years,' recalls George Dunwoody, 'coming home to work on the farm when things eased off during the summer. Cecil Brabazon had been a good amateur but was a highly successful trainer of both flat horses and jumpers. He had some good horses when I was there including Jack Chaucer after which a race, the Jack Chaucer Chase at Leopardstown, is named and I did much of the schooling on him. He also had Pontet who won the Irish National.'

When Thomas Dunwoody died George moved across the border, the majority of his rides coming from trainers based in the north. He began combining training with riding at the tender age of twenty-four and it was a little horse called Desire, who won three times in a week, once on the beach at Laytown, each time with George in the saddle, that gave him the start he needed to get established as a trainer. His career as an amateur saw him competing against Bunny Cox, Kevin Prendagast, Dermot Weld, P. P. Hogan and the late Billy Rooney, to whom he was often runner-up in the Northern Ireland amateur championships. There are only two racecourses in the north, Down Royal and Downpatrick. Consequently, much of George's time was spent travelling to meetings south of the border. He won the Meath Hunt Cup, a prestigious race over banks run in the centre of Navan racecourse, on Highland Ballot for Brigadier Fowler, Aesculus and Vessington Belle for Mrs Gerald St John Nolan, whose Drumroan, some years later, was a fast-finishing third behind Lucius in the 1978 Grand National. Though he never won a La Touche, the big banks race at Punchestown, he won several races over banks there including the Punchestown Cup.

In the late 1950s George was training in County Antrim and had a good bumper horse called Pappa Threeways. 'It was just the type the English liked to come over and buy,' he remembers before pointing out it is still the type of horse that attracts English buyers to Ireland. Looking at the horse with her mother was Epsom trainer's daughter Gillian Thrale.

The pair met again in 1960 at the Punchestown Festival, a two-day meeting, when Arbuoy, a decent chaser trained by George and ridden on this occasion by Pat Taaffe, was beaten by a neck in the Prince of Wales Cup, the feature race on the opening day.

Gillian Thrale was from a well-known southern racing family. Her cousin Peter was a successful trainer and, based just outside Guildford before the Second World War and at Epsom just afterwards, trained for Lord Rosebery among others. Her father, Dick, had been a leading amateur during the 1920s. He rode numerous winners and is reputed to have gone through the card one day at the Old Surrey and Burstow point-to-point. He was noted for his horsemanship and wonderful hands. Much as the Jockey Club do these days when an amateur is seen to be taking away the living of the professionals because he has too many rides, so Dick Thrale, after winning the amateur championship, was given the choice of either easing up on the number of mounts he took as an amateur or turning professional. No-one likes to turn down rides and, as he had won the amateur title, he turned professional.

In 1930 at Lingfield on Friday the thirteenth, the day before his marriage, riding number 13 on the card and at the thirteenth fence he suffered a horrendous fall in which he badly fractured his skull. There were no such things as body protectors in those days, let alone helmets of any kind. He remained unconscious for three weeks, a mild inconvenience for the following day's nuptials. As a result his wedding to Leonora Adlercron was postponed for six months. And, though he rode again following his recovery, it was generally considered he never rode with quite the same dash or urgency and, increasingly, he switched his attention to training.

Leonora, Richard Dunwoody's grandmother, was also a talented horsewoman with a great eye for a horse. She had lived at Plumpton in Sussex and used to divide her time riding out for the late Towser Gosden's father (John Gosden's grandfather), hunting and showing. She had a photographic memory for pedigrees, a subject in which she was very interested, and did a lot of the buying for local trainers and as a female bloodstock agent was something of a pioneer. Women buying horses? In those days the idea was almost inconceivable. Her purchases included Brian Swift's sprinters Tribal Chief and Decoy Boy. She also bought the 1959 Champion Hurdler, Fare Time, as a yearling.

Gillian was born in 1932, an only daughter, and though Dick Thrale had originally started training at Addington, near Croydon, where the family also farmed, he, Leonore and Gillian headed for

Epsom in 1949 and in 1952 took on Downs House, the famous yard which backs on to the mile and a half (Derby) start of the course, now occupied by Philip Mitchell.

Perhaps the most important horse Dick Thrale ever trained was Monaveen. Important, that is, from jump racing's point of view. Owned by Mr Dal Hawkesley, Dick had run him as an eight-year-old in the 1949 Grand National. He had been prominent for a long way before falling with Tony Grantham, whose son Tom rides as a professional today. The race was won by 66–1 outsider Russian Hero and the previously unknown Irish jockey Leo McMorrow.

It so happened at that time that Lord Mildmay and his trainer and great friend Peter Cazalet had finally persuaded the then Queen Elizabeth (now the Queen Mother) that she should own a jumper. Lord Mildmay was one of this century's great amateurs but was jinxed in the National. In 1936 riding his own Davy Jones he had been upsides the winner, Reynoldstown, at the second last when the buckle in his reins had come undone and, unable to steer, Davy Jones had run out at the last. Twelve years later the jinx had struck again; this time up with the leaders three from home on Cromwell, he was attacked by cramp in his neck, the hangover of a broken vertebra he had sustained in a fall at Folkestone. Unable to move on Cromwell he was an unlucky third behind Sheila's Cottage. Whatever his luck as a National jockey we have the enthusiastic Lord Mildmay to thank for introducing racing's greatest and most loved patron to the winter game.

The task of finding a suitable horse for her was not going to be easy. However Tony Grantham, Cazalet's professional jockey, suggested Monaveen was just the ticket. The gelding had been travelling exceedingly well up to the point where he'd fallen in the 1949 National and would be the ideal horse for the following year's race for racing's new royal patron, who was to share him with her daughter, Princess Elizabeth. Sold by Dick Thrale, he won first time out in Royal colours at Fontwell and went on to finish second to Freebooter in the Grand Sefton over the Aintree fences. He went to Liverpool in 1950, winner of his last three races, and was 100–7 joint third favourite in front of one of Aintree's largest crowds who had come to support the King and Queen. He led for a circuit before eventually dropping back to finish fifth to the fifteen-length winner Freebooter. A postscript to this is that when George and Gillian Dunwoody, after a lifetime in racing, retired to live in a small cottage on the Oxfordshire border of the Cotswolds they called the house 'Monaveen'.

Dick Thrale eventually retired from training in 1967 and he and Leonora moved from Epsom to Eastbury, a small village a couple of miles outside of Lambourn. His sprinter Indigenous set the five-furlong course-record at Epsom in 1960, a world record for that distance which still stands to this day.

But back in 1962 the persistence at matchmaking of Stewart and Adare Catherwood, great friends of George Dunwoody and owners of Arbuoy and later the enigmatic Little Bay, eventually paid off when they persuaded Dick's daughter Gillian that she and George ought to get married. The Catherwoods still own horses today, with Gordon Richards, and Richard Dunwoody's rides include their Four Trix and Sandy Braes. Harry Catherwood, Stewart's brother, earned himself the job of best man.

Shortly afterwards, George accepted a job to manage a stud and train privately at Comber, near Belfast, for the late Frank Shane. He had bred the 1958 Derby second, Paddy's Point, and Paddy's Sister. George took up the job in June 1963 but by December Shane had died. With no son or heir, the stud and its horses had to be sold. The Dunwoodys remained at Comber for a further year preparing the horses for the dispersal sale which was to be held at Goffs in Dublin. During this time Thomas Richard Dunwoody was born, at Johnstone House, part of the Royal Victoria Hospital in Belfast, weighing in at 7lb 2oz. It was not an easy birth and Gavin Boyd, one of the top gynaecologists in Northern Ireland who helped deliver him but is now retired, still follows the progress of the baby boy he welcomed into the world on 18 January 1964. 'I'll never forget him coming in and saying that Richard was all right except for one problem,' says Gillian. 'I remember being terrified at what he was about to tell me thinking he would say there was something seriously wrong with Richard. But it was just that he had a mole under his left eye. He said if it had been a girl they would have left it but suggested Richard have it removed when he was old enough, which he did when he was four.'

'We took him to see his grandparents at Downs House, Epsom, for the 1964 Derby,' recalls George. 'We all went to the races and the housekeeper wheeled his pram down the garden towards the racecourse so I suppose you could say Richard watched his first

Derby aged six months.' The race was won by Scobie Breasley on Santa Claus. 'Even aged three Richard would come racing with us,' he adds. 'You couldn't do it with young children now but Richard would get a racecard off Gillian and that would be the last we'd see of him until after the last race when he would come and find us.'

Several years later, Richard was dragging his three-year-old sister Gail around at a point-to-point. They'd run from one vantage point to another, trying to see as many fences being jumped as possible. Running across the course like this during the third race he tripped on a tent peg and landed on another which left a deep gash just above his eye. He was lucky not to have lost an eye but he was taken to Dundonald Hospital for stitches. The scar is still evident just above his eyelid. A busy Saturday afternoon, however, meant he had to wait for half an hour while the doctor attended other casualties. While waiting with a bloody patch over his left eye, Raymond Martin, an amateur jockey, was brought in on a stretcher. He had had a ghastly fall, his lungs had collapsed and had it not been for the continued pumping of his chest by a doctor who hunted with the North Down and had seen what had happened at the fence, he'd have surely died. He was wheeled past the young Dunwoody whose day was turning into one hell of an adventure. He could see Raymond's boots and breeches protruding from blankets so knew it was a jockey. God, how exciting. Not only had he been injured himself, like jockeys, but he'd been brought to the same hospital that injured jockeys were brought. Jeanie Mack, what excitement for the young boy whose own injury had elevated his status, in his own mind at any rate, to nothing short of a hero. Now he was right in the thick of it. Raymond was in a pretty bad way though and making blood-curdling noises, gasping, gurgling and rattling as people with collapsed lungs do.

'They've just brought a dead jockey in,' confided Richard to sister Gail. At this stage Gillian, herself a little queasy at the sight of their friend having to be constantly resuscitated, thought it prudent to take Gail out of the hospital. She was to wait by the car for the stitching, which was clearly going to be delayed a little longer. It was bad enough, Gillian thought as mothers do, that Richard had seen what could happen to jockeys in the real world, she didn't want her daughter to see Raymond in the same state.

As Gail waited patiently she was recognized by a friend, a middle-aged woman, who asked the small girl what was happening. 'They've just brought in a dead jockey,' Gail replied excitedly. Unfortunately her version of events was overheard by Mrs Martin, Raymond's mother, who was waiting anxiously in a car nearby. A happy postscript is that Raymond Martin recovered sufficiently to partner Call Collect to win the Aintree Foxhunters in 1989, the Cheltenham equivalent in 1990 and ride Call Collect in that year's National.

In 1965 the family moved to Kilbright House, a yard and small farm in County Down near the back of Carrowdore Castle on the Down peninsula. It is near the fishing village of Portavogie where they'd land their prawn catches. On a clear day Scotland and the Isle of Man are visible from the long sandy beaches which were ideal for exercising horses, either galloping or trotting through the shallow salt water on a gentle slope. George had not given up his trainer's licence from his days with Frank Shane and began to build up his training interests again. Mrs Thrale, his mother-in-law, found him suitable horses from England and every single one she sent over won.

The owners of Carrowdore Castle, the Mitchells, bred horses, but more importantly their daughters, Elspeth and Fiona, had outgrown a strong little grey pony called Tony, a 12.2 hh Connemara crossed with Welsh mountain. There is nothing like a good pony to get you going. A good teacher, a guide and a safe conveyance, they demonstrate all the qualities of a faithful Sherpa without which Everest couldn't be conquered. The best ones can't be controlled, they do their own thing and you just go with the flow. They prefer hunting to gymkhanas, they follow hounds and not the field master, they lead horses over spooky ditches and awkward hedges. They live turned out in a paddock during the term, get laminitis when the grass is lush, and hunt three days a week in the holidays, and get you in and invariably out of trouble. In your dreams you win the National once a day on them or, if Olympia's on television, you win the puissance. Every cavalletti is Becher's Brook. 'You made it look easy,' says David Coleman thrusting a microphone under your chin. 'It was all the horse,' you modestly answer. My God, we didn't half dream on those ponies. We might say it was West Tip which made Richard. To a certain extent it was but go further back in time, back to the salad days of our Belfast child, and Tony the pony was the real making of Richard Dunwoody, the jockey.

Shortly after Tony's arrival at Kilbright House, Richard would school up over the hurdles behind his father's horses before going to Dunover Primary School for the day. 'I remember John Harty was coming to school one morning,' says George, 'and it happened to freeze the night before. We had been all set to school with Richard before he left for school but the ground was too firm. We decided to delay it until after breakfast. Richard would have to go to school and miss it. However there were ructions. He dug his toes in very firmly, refusing to go to school until he'd schooled Tony.'

Dunover, a small school for the children of local farmers, which numbered about twenty-five pupils, was run by Miss Little and Mrs McIllveen. The former, who suffered from Multiple Sclerosis, died in October 1992 but remained one of Richard's biggest fans until her death and exchanged letters with Gillian Dunwoody every Christmas. Mrs McIllveen still writes. 'Dunover is no longer now,' says Gillian, 'but it provided Richard with a wonderful grounding and when he eventually went to school in England he was a year ahead of his contemporaries.'

Tony, who had arrived when Richard was four, was hunted with the North Down, firmly attached to one of his parents by a leading rein. If George was on a difficult horse then Gillian would lead him from a bicycle. Tony was extremely strong although he was fine in a very enclosed space, like the garden. To the budding jockey the lawn was the perfect surface; that's where he would set up his cavallettis and the lawn was wrecked. As he grew older Richard was allowed to hack to local meets where he'd be met by a parent to be attached to a rein. Tony was a cute little pony and once he knew he was hunting and the hounds had arrived he'd get impossibly stronger.

One particular morning they were meeting outside Dunover Primary. George and Gillian were to meet their seven-year-old son up there in the car but they were delayed and when they arrived the hounds had moved off. Gillian panicked. They didn't see Richard for two and a half hours. They were getting more frantic by the minute. When they did see him he was in the leading half dozen, up among the pink coats of the huntsman Tommy Taylor, and the Masters, in a park. But because they were harriers hunting hares which invariably run in circles, every time they tried to get to Richard, he'd appear the other side of the park. He eventually emerged, his face a darker shade of hunting pink, speechless and exhausted. 'I had to drive him home,' says George, 'and Gillian led Tony home. I tried to ask him how he'd got on, what he'd jumped but there was no answer, he was completely exhausted. Quiet as a lamb. I was worried that he'd been frightened by it. But after he'd had a hot bath he told us everything, never stopped talking about it for days.'

On another occasion Richard's day hunting was cut short after he'd aimed Tony at a flax hole in the ground. In those days when they had cut linseed they would dig a large hole and drown the flax in it. In the winter these holes would be empty of flax but full of stagnant stained water. No sensible horse would have attempted to jump it but Tony, ever the enthusiast behind hounds in full cry and the sound of Tommy's horn, had attempted it. He landed halfway across, and swam out and up the steep sides. He was black except for the grey tips of his ears while Richard was black and soaked up to his neck.

At the same time Richard was getting more involved with the racehorses. George was having some success with horses like Zel, with which he'd won two bumpers, one at Mullingar, the other at Baldoyle (an old Dublin track). Terry Casey, who as a trainer was to supply Richard with Glenrue, his first winner around Aintree in the Topham Trophy, rode Zel to win over hurdles. He was eventually struck into and never got to go chasing although that would have been his forte. Lesson Two, a mare won the Mickey McArdle Memorial Cup at Dundalk while Aldave won eight races over hurdles.

Aged seven Richard led up his first horse, Rotomar Girl, in a race at Gowran Park. 'She was a sensible mare and to go to Gowran was a two-day trip. Instead of taking a lad away I said I'd take Richard. He was leading her round the paddock and Jim Marsh, who now manages the Curragh, was a pretty fierce stipendiary steward in those days. He asked me if it was my boy who was leading the mare round the paddock. "Is he not a bit young?" he added on the point of having me up. But Richard had put on a cap and had made himself look older than he was.'

In 1972 the family moved to England. George had been offered a job by William Reynolds, an American, running Charlton Down Stud, near Tetbury. It backs on to Highgrove. Reynolds had owned Black Satin, third to Humble Duty in the 1970 1,000 Guineas. 'I thought it was a job for life,' recalls George. 'But his wife didn't like the English climate and he sold up and went back to America in the end.'

Richard had moved to Tetbury School. Dunover had set him up with such a good grounding he was put in classes a year ahead of his age group. At the same time he hunted with the Beaufort. Tony the pony had made the trip too and one day their combined boldness and cheek earned him a scolding from Lady Violet Vernon, a noted judge of horses, who rode sidesaddle. She was hunting a brown horse that was hard to hold. When set up for a fence there was no stopping this hunter. Despite Richard being older and stronger Tony was also still unstoppable when aimed at an obstacle. They were both out of control while hounds were running. Lady Violet screamed at Richard to get out of the way at a fence. Tony had other ideas, nipped in front, and Lady Violet's brown hunter nearly landed on top of the little grey pony. When they came to a brief halt she sought out the rude little boy and gave him hell. She did not know who Richard was and asked a friend later. As it so happened her groom had just handed in his notice to go and work at Charlton Down Stud. When she found out that Richard's father ran the place, it was like a red rag to a bull. She went back and gave him another rollocking.

Schooling, of the reading and writing variety, was going well. Though he was treading water for much of his time at Tetbury, he sat a scholarship to Rendcomb College aged ten, passing the entrance exam but failing the scholarship. He was, said the headmaster, too young and so he trod water for a further year, and retook the exam, aged eleven, this time passing. He had been there a year before his parents, who'd been at Charlton Down for five years, decided to move to Newmarket after William Reynolds had announced his intention to manage the place himself before selling.

George took a job riding out for Paul Kelleway. Ben Hanbury, who had ridden for George on occasions in Ireland as an amateur and had trained for Reynolds, and was therefore well known to the Dunwoodys, offered Richard the ride on his hack during the holidays when he heard how mad-keen he was. Eventually Richard progressed to Hanbury's racehorses and then started riding out for Kelleway, a fearless jump jockey who'd turned to training, at Shalfleet on the Bury Road in Newmarket.

During one winter Richard was twice bucked off the same yearling. Each time he'd held on to it, to be legged back up by the trainer.

'Paul came up to me later that day,' says George. 'He said that when lads hit the deck twice like Richard had the colour drained from their faces. "That boy of yours", he said, "never changed colour." '

At the same time George, who'd spent the better part of his lifetime riding chasers, was getting quite a thrill riding Swiss Maid. She was one of several decent fillies in Shalfleet at the time, Madam Gay and Green Girl being other notable females and Star Way a decent colt. 'I used to get a great thrill riding her out,' he says. 'She was a big strong mare. I was a stone heavier than the others and accustomed to riding comparatively slow chasers. She still worked better than anything. She won the Champion Stakes the same day that I'd taken Green Girl to Longchamp for Paul. Green Girl was beaten by a neck. It was nearly a great double.'

When Paul's headlad and George's good friend, Arthur Taylor, moved to Luca Cumani at Bedford House just down the road, he suggested George move with him. Together they could run the second yard and George began breaking and backing Cumani's yearlings. One particular colt had given some difficulty. He had bumped his head and they were having trouble getting a bridle on him. George spent hours patiently getting to know the colt, eventually backing him and riding him away. 'I eventually said to Luca that if he sent the horse to the bottom yard I'd come in during evening stables and look after this horse,' recalls George. It turned out to be Comanche Run, winner of the St Leger and a memorable Irish Champion Stakes at Phoenix Park under Lester Piggott.

Richard passed his O levels with flying colours – of the ten he'd taken, he passed eight with A grades. At Rendcomb, though there were horses for the sixth-form girls, the nearest he came to horses was when he and a few friends would cycle down to Cirencester Park to watch polo. Instead he turned his attention to the school's sports: cricket, in which as wicket keeper he sustained a broken nose; rugger and hockey. His career there was not entirely unblemished. The day after he and two mates, Richard Evans and Tim Pratt, had finished their O levels they took their bikes over to Northleach to one of the boy's homes. They had a few beers there and on the way back bought a couple of bottles of Martini. Richard and Tim were paralytic while Richard Evans passed out on a bank in a field above the school and could not be found. They were suspended for the first week of the following term.

After a year studying Biology, Physics and Chemistry – with a view to becoming a vet – Richard left Rendcomb to spend three months with Paul Kelleway in Newmarket as a pupil assistant, while living at home, and another three with John Bosley at Bampton near Brize Norton in Oxfordshire, a small family-run yard where he lived in the house with the genial trainer's family. From there he went to Captain Tim Forster at Letcombe Bassett near Wantage. He tipped the scales at 8st 7lbs.

CHAPTER TWO

CAPTAIN TIM FORSTER'S YARD in Letcombe Bassett nestles below the church at the foot of Segsbury Hill. The Captain and his humour, dry as the desert, live in the thatched cottage. Marigold Coke is, has been, and for ever will be, secretary at the Old Manor. 'I wish Richard would smile more when he wins,' she said then. She still wishes.

The dark red-painted stable doors in a square yard around a bowling green of a square lawn have welcomed back a thousand winners. The tack room, refuge from the rain, is a scruffy, darkly lit couple of rooms. On wet days smoke billows from the seams of an old stove fed on coke, an incinerator for old scraps of leather, rubbish, cotton wool stained with blood and green oils. A white haze winds its way up to the ceiling between drying horsey-smelling exercise rugs, heavy with rain.

Those thousand winners have made a score or more competent jockeys, professional and amateur. Good horses, they say, make good jockeys. The Captain made Graham Thorner champion in the 1970/71 season, and though his retained jockeys have not risen to quite those heights since, they've invariably done well. This academy takes green, spotty-faced, poorly paid boys straight from school as its raw material. Between the early mornings, stinking mucksacks, dusty straw, long trips to the races with the unoriginally nicknamed experienced lads – Geordie, Ginger, Taffy and Mick as its corporals, the late John Humphries its headlad and sergeant major – the apprentice is knocked into shape, the rough edges rounded. He exits from the Old Manor a few years later, smarter, streetwise, with a contribution to that thousand winners, his confidence boosted but feet firmly on terra firma, ready to seek racecourses paved with gold.

It is not just what the Captain says and does. He'll let the ambitious work out the riding for themselves, he'll let the novice Richard Dunwoody ask Hywel Davies the questions, but he will give him the experience of riding better horses, schooling old handicappers and then young babies.

The Old Manor is an education in life. Survive a couple of winters hammered into shape by Ginger and the boys and you'll come through with a diploma but without your virginity. You're not bullied, but if you're cheeky it'll earn you a thump. To retain an amateur status you're employed as 'pupil assistant' and paid a pittance. But you soon develop the ability to get by on £15 a week, budgeting for expenditure on betting, booze, food and petrol, and accommodating parents help – as you time your last 10p to run out in mid-conversation to your parents, you know a parcel or cheque in the next post is on the cards. Girlfriends buy their own drinks. A racing yard is no bad staging post for anyone brought up in the sheltered environment of a public school.

Richard Dunwoody arrived in December, a fresh-faced, rather intense and easily embarrassed seventeen-year-old who'd prefer to read the form than a comic. It was like the first day at a new school. Dropped off by a friend of the Bosleys he had arrived, on his own for the first time, at the university of life. He moved into a small rented house, Manor Cottage, just across from the church in Letcombe Regis and at various times shared it with Alan Freeman, who worked for the late Matt McCourt, Peter Grady, who now runs a livery yard near Newmarket, Neil Morrice, then Press Association now Lambourn correspondent for the *Racing Post*, and Mick Furlong, a former top Irish jump jockey.

That first short season, from December until May, flew past. The route to Greendown became familiar: up Gramp's Hill, along an old cart track called the Ridgeway which runs from East Anglia to Salisbury Plain but skirts most of the area's training centres, down the side of the schooling ground, up the all-weather gallop or up the turf scattering noisy plover in your wake. God, it could be cold at the top too, it's a wonder there weren't days when you suffered exposure and frostbitten noses instead of the excruciating agony of the blood returning to numbed hands and feet. Then the Captain's instructions would get carried on the wind to another part of the Downs and you'd frantically wonder what you were meant to be doing: cantering, galloping, with whom? You were too afraid to ask.

That December it snowed heavily. For three weeks, from the end of the first week until Boxing Day, racing was abandoned. The Captain's horses trotted round a paddock above Letcombe Bassett's cress beds. Cold hands and fresh horses trotting in mind-numbing circles but plenty to laugh about, one lad hanging off an old chaser that had whipped round at an imaginary bogeyman, another lad on the deck. Then, of course, there were those mornings money can't buy. The turf coated in a crisp, sugary frost, cobwebs hanging in the air, horses breathing white smoke like dragons in the early morning mist. Behind you a clump of beech trees filters the orange sun, a perfect circle, as it rises over the eastern horizon. And you think, how lucky. Had things worked out differently, if you hadn't dreamed of winning the National or storming, head down, up the hill at Cheltenham, you'd still be crawling out of bed, hungover after a night in the college bar, just in time to make first lecture, perhaps a talk on parasitology, unshaven.

The point-to-point season approached. The Captain had a time-honoured link with local farmer and point-to-point trainer the late Colin Nash. He farmed at Kingston Lisle, was Master and huntsman of the Old Berks Hounds. He always had a few home-bred pointers and hunterchasers for which he used to recruit his amateurs from the Captain, give them their first experience. There was mention of the boy Dunwoody having a few rides but that first season time ran out. Richard was unaware that there was a deadline for registering his rider's certificate by the beginning of February. His début would have to be put on hold which was no bad thing. He still had much to learn, was palpably weak and still only weighed 8st 7lb. During the summer break he scanned the racing calendar for amateur races, ringing up for rides and waiting by the phone for replies. Eventually one Sunday morning, August 1982, a Dr Jones rang back. Could Richard ride Mallard Song in the Lysaght Amateur Riders Stakes over two miles at Chepstow on 31 August. You bet he could.

Mallard Song carried 9st 8lb, with Richard's 5lb claim, 9st 3lb. He'd do it with a big saddle. Most of the leading amateurs of the time had rides in the race. Jim Wilson, who eighteen months earlier had won the Gold Cup on Little Owl, was the most experienced. Oliver Sherwood, now training in Lambourn, was to ride Graham Thorner's Brando. William Muir, also a trainer, was on the favourite Champagne Charlie. Peter Hobbs, then an agricultural student at Cirencester, was riding for Peter Cundell, and Charlie Gordon-Watson, now a leading bloodstock agent, had a ride.

The race couldn't have gone much better. The 33–1 outsider Mallard Song finished a two-and-a-half length second to Adrian Sharpe who rode Radfield. Richard had led for a while, was in contention all the way and was beaten by a better horse on the day.

The day didn't end up as well it might have done. On the way back to Letcombe near Swindon, clearly still at Chepstow in his own mind, Richard went a considerable way towards writing off his yellow Morris Marina when he drove up the backside of another car at a roundabout. The car was eventually written off over a bank the following season after he'd picked up a borrowed saddle.

Richard looked after three horses including Our Laurie. In Newmarket he had led up Gay Kelleway on her first winner, Sass, and for the Bosleys had led up Corn Street when he had won. In February he led up in a chase at Towcester. The Captain had three runners and Our Laurie was the outsider at 16–1 but was to be ridden by John Francome. 'John was doing 10st 8lb,' says Richard. 'I was too young and green to notice that he must have passed the saddle out the changing-room window to do that weight!' Now in the 1982/83 season he was joined by another aspiring amateur from the West Country, Luke Harvey, whose humour was to provide a great source of amusement over the next few years.

There were those horses to ride out which bring any champion jockey back down to earth. Professor Plum did two laps of Greendown on several occasions. Once after schooling over three fences he continued, rapidly, towards home. He made it back before the rest of the string but Richard had baled out on the approach to the five-bar gate at the top of the schooling ground. Drumadowney, a talented but quirky front-runner, backed into a telegraph pole and then proceeded to plant himself in a hedge one day. Drumgora, a former two-mile champion chaser, was an old horse with two gears, walk or flat out. The lads sussed that if he went up the gallops in front away from the others he was, at least, holdable. There was vague amusement when Richard said he was going to bring Drumgora up in the string. By the time he had got to the top he was travelling at full speed and the young amateur, his reins in loops, put on the style as he passed the rest of the string. It caused some consternation that he could look so relaxed and posey in a situation which was clearly lost. He completed a two-mile lap before he could pull him up at the foot of the schooling ground from where he had originally set off.

Another time Richard annoyed Ginger on the way home from the gallops with his yappy banter. Ginger, who had a temper to match his red hair, was obviously having a bad day and, instead of waiting until breakfast to sort out Richard, he pulled him clean off his horse on the Ridgeway.

Though he was occasionally allowed to school for the Captain at this stage, it was Colin Nash who asked him to help out with schooling and on 5 February 1983 he offered Richard his first ride over fences at Stratford on Wellands Copse, an experienced hunterchaser who could belt a fence but rarely fell. Richard 'banned' his parents from attending but they made the trip from Newmarket. Every time Richard was led past them in the parade ring they ducked but were convinced they'd been spotted when the Captain came over to chat to them about Richard's progress. Wellands Copse and Richard finished sixth of seventeen in the Credit Call Cup. In his rides record it says 'finished tired', he's not sure whether this refers to himself or the horse.

His second ride, Gambling Ghost, unseated him at Leicester at the end of the month when he might have been second, but it was Wellands Copse which provided him with his first placed ride, third, later that afternoon at the all-hunterchase meeting. However, and there's hope for us all, Richard hit the deck four times in his first eight rides that spring. Though Wellands Copse had also unseated him, it was Gambling Ghost who was providing the most sport. 'I'm not sure even now I'd be able to get him round,' says Richard. 'He took a long time to get his jumping sorted out.'

His sixth ride, at Fontwell, provided him with his first proper fall, not just an unseating. We all remember our first falls especially if we've been unseated a couple of times first. You've been blooded and muddied, in the thick of the action, and if you come out unscathed like you did every time you practised it off the sofa as a dreamy child, it gave you great confidence that falling would not hurt every time. 'I was over the moon that I'd got away with it,' says Richard. 'It was almost as if I'd ridden a winner.' It is a strange philosophy. I don't suppose racing drivers feel the same about their first crashes.

The first winner came on Colin Nash's mare Game Trust at Cheltenham's all-hunterchase evening meeting on 4 May 1983. It was Richard's twelfth ride over fences. Always amongst the leaders he took up the running at the third-last fence, survived a blunder at the last fence to win the Bramley Novices' Hunters' Chase.

David Nugent's Ballydonagh provided the next winner at Ludlow eight days later while Gambling Ghost finally repaid him for those early falls with success at Newton Abbot the following week. *Sporting Life* noted he was a 'name to keep in mind for next season'. The *Sporting Chronicle* pointed out it was a 'polished display'. With a regularity for visiting the winner's enclosure that he has kept up ever since, the Captain's Swordsman, the first ride for his guv'nor and his first ride against professionals, gave him his fourth winner of his twenty-three first-season rides, at Fontwell. Going to scale at 9st 7lb was now a struggle. To this he had added a brace of point-to-point successes, on Game Trust at the Old Berks and Gambling Ghost at the Hampshire Hunt.

The 1983/84 season began with a winner, Chelsea Bar at Devon in August. 'Stuck to the rails like an old hand' reported one paper. 'Again demonstrated undoubted promise' said *Sporting Life*. In October, Arthur Barrow put him up on the 1980 Gold Cup winner Master Smudge to claim 7lbs from his top-weight and the pair finished seventh.

Until an amateur has ridden seventy-five races against professionals he is free. After that, though it goes into the Jockey Club's administration fund, an owner is charged for his services like any professional. It is a system to help get an amateur going, gives him a leg up. However it is open to abuse. If you have a rotten horse with no earthly chance of winning why pay for a pro when you can have an amateur for free? Simple logic. Dunwoody's comments on Pat O'Connor's ex-Irish Alpine Highway who fell at Southwell make interesting reading. 'Hywel [Davies] had him at livery. Schooled him 2 days before – jumped well. Different horse on the course. Keen start. Jumped first off forehand, ran very free to second. Galloped into bottom of it. Rubber bit – no use, didn't respond. Unfortunate there was such a fast pace. Heard afterwards – completed once in 12 outings.' Ever since he has always looked up a horse's form before accepting a ride on it.

His twenty-sixth ride that season was Hal's Joy for a certain Martin Pipe who was starting to have a few winners. 'Had him on outer – to orders,' wrote Richard with some frustration. 'Could have had him on inner.' Hal's Joy finished fourth beaten four lengths. His next ride for Pipe was on Corporal Clinger at Plumpton. He thought it would be his last after being beaten half a length by Martin Bosley, his future best man.

The rides were coming thick and fast for an amateur but the winners seemed hard to come by after his good start to the season. He had to wait until Boxing Day for his third winner – Silent Tango for Alan Blackmore who was another of his regular patrons in the early days. However there was a sting in the tail when the stewards disqualified him from first to fourth and suspended him for two days for careless riding. He had been unable to use his whip in his left hand and had consequently bumped the third, who in turn bumped the fourth, up the run-in. Though he had four rides that day the others had disappointed. It was one of those days – and champion or beginner, 'those days' will stick with you until the day you retire.

As a promising claimer he was nevertheless being offered some decent rides in some hot races including Spinning Saint, Roadster, Oyster Pond and Memberson. The winners flowed again and following a seven-day rest for concussion he began to benefit from a fall suffered by the Captain's then jockey, Hywel Davies, at Doncaster in February. Riding Solid Rock Davies had the fall we all dread, drilled and milled into the ground. He had stopped breathing and owed his life to a doctor who happened to be standing by the fence. But Richard really announced his arrival as a future champion with a four-timer at Hereford on 3 March. Hurry Up Henry finished third in the first,

Mrs Tucker's Pucka Fella won the next, the Captain's Toy Track won the novices' chase beating Baron Blakeney who went on to win at Liverpool, Spinning Saint won the handicap chase for Kim Bailey, while Bob Champion's Three Chances landed the hunterchase.

Going out for the hunterchase Kim Bailey had, jokingly, said that should Richard win it, and thus have his claim reduced to 4lbs, then he wouldn't be allowed to ride Mister Bee for him in the last. Ironically Mister Bee was beaten a neck in the last by Ben de Haan riding a horse of Fred Winter's.

Michael Oliver's brother Martin had already noticed Richard riding and suggested he ride a few for the yard. It began with Bashful Lad and in the Midlands Grand National at Uttoxeter in April, where he rode a double for the Captain, he partnered the novice seven-year-old West Tip to finish ninth, one place incidentally behind Little Polveir. Both were destined to win the Grand National.

The Captain and Richard decided that he should have a crack at winning the amateur championship following his late flourish though he had left his run a shade too late. The following season he would turn professional and ride under Hywel Davies as second jockey to Captain Forster. He finished the season, third in the championship behind Simon Sherwood (28 winners) with 24 winners from 210 rides.

Progress towards the top has been a steep upward curve ever since. The 1984/85 season saw him win the Mecca Bookmakers Hurdle at Sandown in January. Michael Oliver's Von Trappe, a horse that did as much as any to promote Richard's career, enormously talented but with no respect for obstacles, continued to demonstrate both sides of his character. At Cheltenham he slid on his belly at one fence but stood up, Richard sat tight and they went on to finish second. Freight Forwarder had also won the same day but it was his recovery on Von Trappe that was televised, after which he was interviewed. West Tip won the Anthony Mildmay Peter Cazalet Memorial at Sandown and he and Von Trappe both went on to win at the Cheltenham Festival, two of the forty-six winners he was to ride that season. Although 13–2 favourite for the Grand National, West Tip fell when going extremely well upsides in front at Becher's Brook second time. Richard had also been second-retained behind Peter Scudamore, ironically yet to ride his first Festival winner, to ride for David Nicholson and spent the summer as a member of the British jump jockeys team to tour America, Australia and New Zealand with Graham Bradley, Steve Smith-Eccles, Hywel Davies and Scu. It was an eye-opening tour. Aged twenty-one he had never travelled abroad before and had to apply for a passport before he could go anywhere. A winner at Fair Hill in America was to sow some productive seeds for the future.

The following season, 1985/86, his fifty-four other winners were eclipsed by West Tip's Grand National victory but again he had some notable rides on Von Trappe. In April, after Scu had announced his intentions to ride for Fred Winter, a position not filled since John Francome had retired the previous season, Richard accepted the job to ride the following season as first jockey for David Nicholson at Condicote. The summer saw him ride the American-trained Flatterer finishing second in the French Champion Hurdle. 'He was possibly the best hurdler I ever sat on,' says Richard. 'It was the hottest day I have ever ridden on and Dawn Run was about a length in front of me when she fell. She looked to have a simple fall but tragically she broke her neck. It was one of Irish racing's saddest days, she'd become the only horse to win the Champion Hurdle and Gold Cup and was almost on a par with Arkle in Ireland. I remember Scu falling twice in the race too, on Gaye Brief. He fell first at the practice fence and again in the race proper. The French Champion Hurdle is one race I will never forget.'

The 1986/87 season was his first with Nicholson at Condicote. At one stage Scu was going to be allowed to keep the ride on Very Promising, the Duke's best horse. So when Very Promising provided the new team with their first big winner in the Mackeson, beating Half Free two lengths, it cemented the partnership. He followed it up with a Black and White Chase victory over Bobsline in Ireland. 'He was a smashing, bouncy athlete,' says Richard with genuine affection. 'He was placed three times in the Champion Chase and had some notable run-ins with Pearlyman. He is still used as a hack at the Duke's.' David Murray-Smith's Church Warden won the H & T Walker Chase while Charter Party, a slow learner, gave him a 'good few burials' including one in The Thinker's Gold Cup.

Kribensis came on the scene in the 1987/88 season and combined with Charter Party to give him the Triumph Hurdle–Gold Cup double on the last day of that year's Festival. It was not before he had received the worst of Christmas presents though. A spill from L'Ane Rouge at Leopardstown's Christmas meeting gave him a heavy landing on his head though he rode Very Promising there. He had more rides at Cheltenham's New Year meeting but his injuries were jarred when he received a smack in the face at the start and was forced to pull up after jumping the first. It meant three weeks out.

During the summer with Martin Bosley as best man he married Carol Abraham in Wantage and they spent their honeymoon in Jersey – racing. Carol had her first ride on her honeymoon! 'It is always hard to get away from racing,' Richard says. 'Even on your honeymoon. I have ridden Jersey every summer since 1986. I even managed to win the Jersey Derby.'

Waterloo Boy was novice chasing during the 1988/89 season and he wound up by winning the Arkle Chase at the Festival. Richard's 91 winners, following 79 and 70, again showed a progression and again secured him third place in the title race which Scu was beginning to monopolize. This was the record-breaking year in which Scu rode 221 winners, 158 of which were for Martin Pipe.

The 1989/90 season began well in America when Highland Bud won the Breeders' Cup Chase although three days earlier Richard had suffered concussion at Ascot. He had spoken to the doctor, as you're required to do after a fall, and the moment was recorded on television but he cannot remember anything from that last ride to when he emerged from a sauna later that day. He was lucky not to be off for a week. Ascot had provided 'one of those days' which demonstrates how we should take nothing for granted in this sport. Sir Jest, something of a character, had refused at the last fence when left in front after Scu had run out with Huntworth, Slieve Felim had fallen and was put down, while Red Procession had buried him at the last fence and given him the concussion.

He had also begun riding for Nicky Henderson as well as Nicholson. Simon Sherwood had retired and Richard now had the ride on Desert Orchid who won the King George VI Chase and the Irish National at Fairyhouse. Kribensis won the Champion Hurdle, Bigsun, looking every inch another National horse, won the Ritz Club Chase and Won't Be Gone Long led the field home up that painfully long run in at Aintree in the John Hughes Memorial over the National fences.

He cracked the 100 winners for the first time at Stratford in May and went on to record his best total, again, 102.

Desert Orchid again won the King George in the 1990/91 season. Remittance Man, an average-looking hurdler, was turning into a very exciting novice chaser and followed in Waterloo Boy's footsteps with a convincing success in the Arkle. Richard had been a warm favourite to win the jockey's championship after Scu broke his leg in a fall at Market Rasen, but Scu recovered and caught up Richard, who'd overtaken him during his recuperation. Although Richard stayed with Scu through April, the stewards knocked his challenge on the head when Col Bill Whitbread and Mrs Cath Walwyn appealed about the result of a race he'd won at Wincanton. Their Kilbrittain Castle, having his last race, had been squeezed out by Came Down on the run-in. At the appeal in Portman Square, Richard was stood down for six days for careless riding. At the time he was a couple of winners behind Scu but his 127 winners were fourteen short of the champion's final score.

The headlines around Christmas 1991, halfway stage for the 1991/92 season, revolved around which ride Richard would select in the King George VI: Desert Orchid, who had provided him with two wins in the race but who appeared to be coming to the end of a glorious career, or the talented Remittance Man, unbeaten but unproven over the trip of three miles. After much heart-searching and what seemed the most important decision of his career he remained faithful to Desert Orchid who fell at the third last. However, Remittance Man could only finish third to The Fellow so his decision had not cost him his third King George. The same happened at Cheltenham, Jamie Osborne stepping in for two Henderson winners, Flown and Remittance Man, and another regular mount Nomadic Way. That year's Liverpool was a meeting of huge contrasts. In three days he rode four winners, including Morley Street, Remittance Man, Carobee and The Antartex who gave him a faultless ride in the John Hughes, and had six fallers. The Jockey Club doctor was keen to stand him down for three weeks following such punishment. Indeed he could scarcely walk to the car park after the last race. However, he persuaded the doctor he was not as bad as that and was back riding again at Ascot the following Wednesday.

Once again he had, as he has every season so far, increased his tally of winners – to 137. For the third consecutive season he had finished runner-up to Peter Scudamore who was winning the championship for the eighth time. The quest for the championship would have to wait another season.

CHAPTER THREE

MUST BE A HELL of a life, that of a jockey. Ride for ten months a year and get paid for doing so. All those winners. All right, you weigh that up against the odd fall but then when do you ever see a top jockey hurt? You get wet and go without supper once a week, but the good days make up for the bad ones, don't they? Then you've two months on the beach in the summer, barbecues and chilled beers, the best of the weather and the most you have to do is mow the lawn, what more could you want? Money for nothing? This is life on the bright side of the road.

Sure, it's a high perch to fall from if you drop out of the top dozen. If Providence, like a fat lollipop lady, guides you across to the dimly lit side of the street where the bogeyman loiters in the shadows. It's tougher at the bottom in this sport, probably is in any sport. You can ride for only six months a year when there's a surfeit of spare rides, but you can't afford to spend the other six months on the beach. The horses you're asked to partner are Dunwoody's or Scudamore's rejects and the falls outweigh the winners. You're fodder for the cannon, a fool rushing in where angels fear to ride. It is a futile heroism that barely pays the mortgage, doesn't constitute a living. But who cares? It's good for the sport, so the cynics say, when a no-hoper rides a winner, makes a good story when a hard-working unknown wins the Grand National or fulfils Warhol's prediction that we're all famous for fifteen minutes. But with Richard Dunwoody, we're talking top jockey and two months solid holiday, aren't we? The National Hunt season usually concludes at the end of May, or the first Saturday in June. It is tradition now, an afternoon meeting at Stratford and an evening meeting at Market Rasen. More often than not all championships have been decided for some time and there is an end of term buzz of excitement. We're married to this sport but there comes a time when we all need a break from our wives. The season usually starts up again on the last Saturday of July, perhaps the first weekend in August at Bangor-on-Dee. Give or take a couple of days that's a two-month recess.

There is much to be done in that period. It is no holiday. Would-be champions are in demand, their presence is much requested. Could Richard present the prizes at the local Pony Club show? Could he open a betting shop? Could he ride at Finmere Show in a charity showjumping event and in an Animal Health Trust charity event at Ascot? At this level you are a high-profile ambassador for the sport. You can't just say no. Then, of course, there are the things you couldn't do during the winter, like visiting the dentist. The only time a jockey gets to go to the dentist in the winter is if he's had his teeth kicked out. A horse's aluminium-plated hoof does the job somewhat quicker than a dentist but its craftwork tends to be somewhat more haphazard. And yet, how often do we see jockeys riding with gum shields? A couple of the girls perhaps. Otherwise never.

But you'd think come Stratford, come the end of the season, come the wilting of the wisteria, the wilting of the hysteria when Cheltenham next season seems so much closer than Cheltenham this season, that the body of the jump jockey would be put out to grass, so to speak. The body protector hung up neatly to gather dust and pollen from the flower display on the kitchen table, the breeches ironed and neatly folded away, the goggles polished, the saddles oiled, the boots sent away for repair. Rolling stones gather no moss and would-be champions are rolling stones. Even the 'holidays' at a would-be champion's level are helter-skelter, hell for leather.

JUNE

So let the Champion's diary begin, not in early August but in early June 1992. The 1991/92 season's just ended, Party Politics won the National, Cool Ground won the Gold Cup and Royal Gait took hurdling's top prize. Desert Orchid bowed out of racing in the King George in the style of a gymnast mistiming a vault. Scudamore's beaten our would-be champion 175 winners to 135, a margin of forty. Richard's satisfied though, it's his personal best total, beating the previous season by ten. Were the championship decided on prize-money he'd have won. He leaves Stratford intact but limping – he'd won one on Four Trix but Scu had matched it and more, he had won two – not to go home but to drive on to Market Rasen, the last 300 miles of a 45,000 mile season, for three more rides. Is it really worth it, on the last day? The answer is one word, 'dedication' – it's why you and I are not champions or anything near it – despite the results, a last and two second lasts.

Richard's left knee, the cause of his limp, has been aggravating him for the last three months of the campaign. It's nothing he couldn't ride with but it's uncomfortable. He's seen Mike Foy, an RAF surgeon whose work at the Ridgeway Hospital, Wroughton is bringing him into regular contact with jockeys, a couple of times. He'd decided on a minor operation. The following Tuesday, first of the 'hols', he drives himself to the Ridgeway. Most Lambourn jockeys know the place. The nurses, familiar faces, greet your arrival. If you were in a coma at Wolverhampton General you'd still request a transfer to the Ridgeway. The operation, an arthroscopy – keyhole surgery – requires a full anaesthetic and leaves three small, insignificant skin punctures. Nothing a few sutures won't darn together.

Jockeys hate hospitals, they're hopeless, hapless patients. A jockey hasn't lived until he's woken up in one, his last recollection the approach to the open ditch. That clinical smell makes you feel faint. You wake up groggy. I'm going to shoot that trainer, you think to yourself, telling me it jumped well. Then you move each limb to see what and what isn't movable or still connected to the nervous system. You might have a broken leg but you can move your hand. That's a relief you think, it could have been worse. You might have two broken legs and you think to yourself, 'When's my next good ride? Will I be riding in time for Cheltenham in three weeks' time?' You're not going to walk out of the place for a month but you still wonder if Mary Bromily, your physiotherapist, will have time to see you in the morning.

Sometimes you've felt so bad that getting to hospital has been a relief. You've been glad to get there, get out of the hands of the volunteers standing by the fence. They're great, do it in all weathers but no matter how good the intentions, if you've only been taught to treat nose bleeds and bee stings, it's not much help when your patient is lying there with broken vertebrae. The jockey arrives the blooded sportsman – your name after all appears in the daily papers – injured in the line of duty, and the geriatric in the bed next door backed you when you won the Grand National. But it doesn't take you long to realize that the everyday heroes are the doctors and nurses. Probably paid less than you are, up all night, answering your moans and your incessant ringing on the alarm.

First reactions are to want to get out the place. And so, still groggy from anaesthetic, Richard stumbles around in his pyjamas, tries to discharge himself, wants to book a taxi home. Carol's riding out, so eventually a nurse calls up George and Gillian Dunwoody who pick him up and he's home in time to see Dr Devious win the Derby. He's ridden by John Reid, a fellow Ulsterman and neighbour.

Thursday, recovered, it's back to hospital, this time Frenchay, near Bristol, to visit Nigel Coleman. Nigel had slipped up on a bend at Worcester, a bit of crowding, lush grass and down you go. As if obstacles didn't cause enough problems. Nigel was concussed but tests revealed no long-term damage and he was discharged. A couple of days later he goes down with a stroke. He spent his thirty-second birthday paralysed down one side and unable to communicate. There but for the grace of God goes every licensed jockey. Call it an occupational hazard if you like. The boys will rally round, fund-raising cricket matches, auctions, dances to see him on his way. And of course don't forget the Injured Jockeys Fund. But when you see Nigel you realize this is one fall from which he'll never completely recover. This is the downside to living on the edge, occasionally somebody slips, loses their footing, like Vivian Kennedy, Philip Barnard, Jayne Thomson and Michael Blackmore. Others, like Jessica Charles-Jones and Sharon Murgatroyd, have become tangled in the safety netting, alive and inspirations to us all, but with broken bodies.

Sunday is spent with Jennifer and Tim Collins near Bicester. They own Remittance Man, champion two-mile chaser. A good relaxed lunch with Nicky and Diana Henderson, they wander down the field to see Remittance Man in holiday mode and Tudor Fable, for whom high hopes are held for the coming season. We all have to sell ourselves these days and off-season lunches are a matter of course. During the two months he'll probably have lunch or dinner with owners, like the Deeleys who own Waterloo Boy, and trainers on half a dozen occasions. It is easy and relaxing to pop down to the local, the Star in Sparsholt, for a bite with Richard Phillips, who's about to take the plunge and give training a go. He has invited along John Inverdale, presenter of the BBC's Sport on Five, to see if he is serious about being a potential owner. The next day Richard drives to Ab Kettleby to see Desert Orchid at Jimmy Burridge's home. The artist commissioned to paint the 'official' Desert Orchid portrait, Richard Dunwoody up, needs more photos.

June and July are also the months in which jump jockeys tend to get married. There tend to be several invitations every summer. This time it is Ian Lawrence and it is preceded by an evening spent at his stag party, held at The Ibex in Chaddleworth, a local pub owned by former jump jockey Colin Brown. It has the Desert Orchid bar. Richard's own stag party in 1988 was held at a London restaurant named School Dinners. Ian, a jockey who spends his summers earning a crust as a valet at flat meetings, is marrying Joe Mercer's daughter, Sarah, and a coach has been organized to pick up his ultimately unruly guests to save them driving. A long night ends up with Ian dyed black.

A course of physiotherapy on the repairing knee must also begin. Richard drives over to Baydon to see Mary Bromily for the first of what will be many sessions during the coming twelve months. The season ticket is booked.

Richard has represented the jockeys on the overnight declaration of jockeys which will come into action for the new season. There is a final meeting of the Jockey Club committee at their headquarters, 42 Portman Square, on 11 July. Richard drives Michael Caulfield, secretary of the Jockeys Association and neighbour, up to London for the meeting and then returns, via the Ridgeway Hospital to have his stitches removed. Michael is the son of the eminent judge Sir Bernard Caulfield but, on leaving Ampleforth, spent the next five years working as a stablelad. The pair met up at Captain Forster's.

They talk racing politics and listen to an Irish band called the Saw Doctors on the way up, both are big fans.

Two weeks ago the season ended. We've hardly had time to catch our breath. A week in Cyprus is booked and the flight leaves on Monday but it's a hectic weekend. Carol is riding Hebridean in a ladies' race at York. He is favourite having run well in a Listed race last time out and Carol is nervous. Richard may ride in Gold Cups as a matter of course but this is her first televised ride and with a surname like hers there are sure to be people watching. She has about five rides a year but, like all lady riders, finds it is a struggle and very competitive to get rides in the few amateur races that there are. Even the surname doesn't help. The Princess Royal, who rides out occasionally at Condicote, is also riding in the race. Carol and Richard walk the course with Hebridean's owner Peter Deal, Newmarket trainer Michael Bell, and his wife Georgina who is also riding. The ground is firm. It is one of the rare occasions when Richard can socialize at the races and he spends much of the afternoon with Peter Deal. Carol finishes fourth, somewhat disappointingly – the ground was too firm for Hebridean. Mrs Dunwoody is cross with herself – she let the Princess up her inner!

Cyprus is hot and relaxing. The Dunwoodys have a hotel room overlooking the marina where Simon McNeill and Martin Bosley, two fellow jockeys, are staying on a yacht with respective partners. There can't be many sports where you go on holiday with your rivals but this is further evidence of the camaraderie behind the weighing room's closed doors. Richard spends an hour each day in the hotel gym exercising his knee with weights. Other forms of exercise include tennis, swimming and highly competitive table tennis tournaments. The knee is in good enough shape for some water-skiing and the winds off Cyprus whip up the sea to the point where it is only just skiable but the speedboat drivers are game for some sport. Richard is well known for being able to take everything a horse can throw at him but if you want to see him brought down put him on a boat on a choppy sea. By his own admission he is not a good sailor. Despite being violently seasick for a day his weight has already gone up to 10st 10lb stripped.

There have been some memorable summer holidays in the past. Some of the worst falls have been off the 'banana', an inflated tube that carries six people and which is towed at high speeds behind speedboats, and the 'ringo', an inflated inner tube, also towed behind a boat. In Zante, Paul Croucher, a late great friend and jockey who was killed in a car accident, was star of that show. He stole the rep's moped one evening and drove off the hotel veranda down a six-foot drop into the sea. He emerged, slowly, and the retrieved moped was never quite the same again. On another occasion, while everyone else hired their own moped, Paul went for the powerful trials bike, which, over-revving up a bank, he succeeded in getting it to do a back flip. Poor old Paul, he's much missed but there's a race run in his memory at Newbury each spring.

Following their return, Richard makes his annual pilgrimage to the Curragh for the Irish Derby. It coincides with the Bellewstown meeting at which he hopes to have a few rides. Because of the huge crowds attending the rematch of the Epsom Derby run between St Jovite and Dr Devious, he gets no further than the hospitality of trainer Mick O'Toole and his son Ciaran, Richard's agent for his Irish rides. Ciaran stays at Hyperion House for Cheltenham. He used to be assistant to David Nicholson and was responsible for getting Richard his first ride as an amateur for the Duke, Sir Gordon, when one of his jockeys was injured. They watch St Jovite run away with the Derby on television before turning up at the course for the post-race picnics.

JULY

July is beginning and so to Bellewstown, a small racing festival threequarters of an hour north of Dublin. It is a very sharp track on top of a hill – it has no comparison this side of St George's Channel – and is reached along long winding lanes. They no longer race over fences there, just hurdles and on the flat. They race three days a year at Bellewstown and its facilities, although not the worst, are not the best. It is a notorious track for horses slipping up, more so than Taunton, even though the bends have been cambered. Richard's four rides at the meeting are the first of eighteen he has before he starts his assault on the British Championship. He has his first fall since the operation on Wicket Keeper. The gelding rears at the start and slips over. He twice slips during the race although he manages to stay on his feet this time. It is a hairy reintroduction.

Following Bellewstown, Richard visits Pat Flynn's yard at Carrick-on-Suir to see Montelado, on whom he had won at the Cheltenham Festival four months previously. They meet Pat and owner Ollie Hannon for lunch and afterwards wander, what seems like miles, across the fields to see the horse.

It's a struggle to do 10st 6lb to ride Jacinto's Boy for Homer Scott at Roscommon. The weight is gradually coming off, much of it in the sauna at the Apprentice School on the Curragh, where Christy Roche, St Jovite's jockey and at that time involved in a High Court action to prevent the Irish Turf Club from enforcing a ban on him, is also sweating. He beats Conor O'Dwyer a shorthead. Conor had dropped him and Ciaran off the previous night and may now be regretting it. Richard blows hard after the race. 'I needed the exercise more than the horse,' he quips. It doesn't take long to lose condition in this sport.

After the annual dentist's visit Richard drives to Checkenden near Reading for a polo lesson with David Heaton-Ellis. There's a charity game, jockeys versus eventers, there the following Saturday. Half the original team of Richard, Jamie Osborne, Carl Llewellyn and myself, has been wiped out in a pile-up riding in a chase in Russia, seven horses having fallen independently at the same obstacle. Carl had suffered multiple bruising which had resulted in a trip to Pyatigorsk Hospital in a push-started ambulance and I had damaged a knee. Substitutes Jamie Railton and Martin Bosley are roped in as last-minute replacements.

The eventers had experience on their side and won by two goals. Richard spends one chukka being run away with by one particular pony. The harder he pulls, the harder it pulls and the worse its steering. He fails to connect stick with ball in that chukka. It is Richard's second competitive game of polo, the first had been against Newmarket trainers a year before when he had ridden Brod Munro-Wilson's best 'Cartier' ponies. No wonder Richard looked good at the game, those ponies were trained to follow the ball and line themselves up for the shots. An eventful day at Checkenden is rounded off at the West Indian cricketer Courtney Walsh's testimonial dinner held at Stowell Park, Northleach, in Gloucestershire.

Next week Richard is up in front of the beaks at Newton Abbot on a speeding charge. His colleagues have little sympathy. He had been in a hurry between Hereford and Newton Abbot, making sure he got there to ride Acre Hill in a walkover at the end of the previous season. He's fined and banned for a fortnight, the first week of which he is to spend in a villa he and Carol have been lent in Portugal. It's an inconvenience though. He has to pay a driver to take him schooling near Stroud for Graham Roe, the first session of the impending season. The pupil requiring an introduction is scatty and he's not so sure it was such a good idea after all. It is reluctant, small, uncomfortable and goes backwards faster than it goes forwards but ends up jumping reasonably. The day after it is off to Jersey for three rides.

The last week of the holiday is truly busman's. A week at the Galway Festival on the west coast of Ireland, six days of racing, eight rides. Galway is an undulating right-handed course and one of the few in Ireland with its own sauna which makes doing the weight easier. You jump a fence by the weighing room, bear right, along past some houses, down a dip, over two fences close together, about seven strides apart in the valley bottom and then face a long climb to the winning post. There is a carnival atmosphere about the Galway Festival, the centre of the course is home for a fun fair. The weighing room looks out over the paddock and winners' enclosure and up towards the stands on top of the hill. It is more relaxed than most British meetings and attended by a number of British-based jockeys, Peter Scudamore, Robert Bellamy, Norman Williamson, many of whom were staying with John and Erna Walsh on the Salthill side of town.

Four Trix, owned by Stewart Catherwood and trained by Gordon Richards, runs third in the Galway Plate which is worth £22,100 to the winner. It's a creditable effort over a trip, two and three-quarter miles, which is well short of his best. He's beaten thirteen lengths by the winner, The Gooser, who is ridden by Adrian Maguire. Cock Cockburn ran a disappointing race in the Galway Hurdle. A well-backed favourite he finished well down the field after blundering at the first flight of hurdles. The race over before it had really begun. Both races are hectic to ride in, fiercely competitive despite the time of year and fast ground. Everyone wants to get a decent prize under their belt.

While most of the other British jockeys return home to commence battle at Bangor and then Newton Abbot, Richard and Norman Williamson stay out to battle out the finish up the hill at Galway on Saturday, 1 August in a valuable hurdle. Norman beats him threequarters of a length. The gamble had nearly paid off, besides which he's missed little at either of the two British meetings.

CHAPTER FOUR

AUGUST

THEY'RE OFF. THE BRITISH 1992/93 National Hunt season has started at Bangor on the last day of July, a Friday, without Richard Dunwoody. It has moved on, like the start of one of winter's long-distance chases, at a sedate pace to the West Country, ice-creams, sunburned holiday crowds browned off by the beach, screaming children and caravan conventions. Scudamore's already on the score sheet, a double at Newton Abbot on the first Saturday in what is a new year for jumping enthusiasts. There was a time before Dunwoody's when jump racing, like a circus or a pub cricket team, went on tour in the West Country. Devon and Exeter, Newton Abbot, Taunton and Buckfastleigh. All that remains of the latter is a weighing room-shaped tin-roofed hut in a hayfield beside the A38; the dual carriageway presumably dissects the old course.

Summer jump racing, in those pre-motorway days, was the prerogative of the west. These courses were rarely used in the winter and, as a consequence, boasted wonderful, spongy turf that never became firm, even in a drought. Now, in August, they're still recovering from the hammering they took in the heavy last New Year's Day, when fields of fifteen left hock-deep hoof prints and gang-banged the turf. Jockeys booked into the Palace in Torquay for the month, now they leave home two and a half hours before they're due to ride.

To all intents and purposes, Richard's British season begins in a bath, someone else's bath at that. After a late night in Galway he has arrived back at Heathrow on Sunday morning. He is picked up by Carol and they drive to the christening of former jockey-turned-trainer Richard Rowe's son, also called Richard. 'Rowsie' retired the previous season. He lives near Findon in Sussex. He just decided one morning when struggling to lose weight on an exercise bicycle that he didn't want to go to Fontwell. Click, just like that. Realized after a career of wasting, winning and being walloped into the ground – and by God he had some falls – that crash dieting wasn't worth it, that there was more to life than denying oneself food, denying oneself a life. It does your brain in eventually. Resilience is like a sculptor's block of stone, the sweating and consequent thirst chips, chips away. The sculptor's creating this wonderful figure and then he chisels out one chip too many and the whole thing shatters. Richard is to be godfather to Rowsie's eldest son. He weighs 10st 3lb and on Monday he must ride at 10st. If you arrived at any other christening in the country and asked to spend an hour and half in the bath first, you'd imagine it might attract some funny looks. Rowsie knows. His family, relations, they know what it's like. This is when he's glad he's a trainer. He may have other worries but he can have a bath, a sauna, when he feels like it not when the job dictates. So remember this is day minus-one, the Sunday before it all begins for the would-be champion, the quiet before the storm, and he's already turning his back on the tasty looking finger buffet. All for what?

For three rides at Newton Abbot. It's an inauspicious start. Sixofus is beaten out of sight, fifty and threequarter lengths according to the form book, in the novices hurdle. Even the form book doesn't record how far Easter Lee is beaten despite being the pick of the paddock and Seven Sons trails in seventy-seven and a half lengths and about half a minute behind the winner, Galway Star, in his handicap hurdle. It is four-nil to Scu by the end of the day. Two days later Rare Bid gets Richard off the mark at Exeter. A juddery start maybe but we're off.

August racing is characterized by concrete ground and small fields of four, five and six runners at meetings held on alternate days – not many horses can withstand the jar of this summer ground on already stretched tendons. For jockeys this isn't the relentless day-in-day-out of mid-winter but is like running in a new engine, gently does it. Winabuck wins at Worcester. Winabuck has earned a certain notoriety for himself, he's not a great jumper. He's not the sort you'd relish riding round Aintree, though he did complete at Cheltenham later in the season. At some stage Winabuck has brought most of his regular riders down to earth with a thump. You wonder whether he forgets what he's meant to do at a fence, has a brainstorm or is unathletic. He seems to jump well on the bridle, when going easily within himself, but then he's fallen on those occasions too. Of course, a fall leads to a loss of confidence and the whole thing spirals downwards like the staircase in a lighthouse.

SEPTEMBER

Richard is becoming edgy. He may have had six winners already (Peter Scudamore had four on 1 September alone) but he's not had a proper fall since mid-April when Al Hashimi contributed to breaking a ditch at Ascot – kept the fence builders employed for a day or two. He's well aware of the law of averages. No falls for five months, you don't begin to think fate is slipping, becoming lackadaisical, inefficient, or drooping like a plant in need of water. No, you look carefully round every corner looking for the booby traps, expecting fate to jump out at you, drag you down five times in a week just to even the scores up. Jockeys don't like going too long without a fall.

Someone watered the thirsty plant at Waregem on 1 September all right, in all senses. Waregem is home of the Grande Steeple de Flanders, the Belgian Grand National. It's a sharp right-handed course, less than a mile round, a cinder trotting track in the centre, and the fences are very different from ours, more like the cross-country phase of a one-day-event: banks, oxers, post and rails, hedges, open ditches, a spectacular gaping water jump in front of the grandstand. It once had one of the worst pile-ups you have ever seen when two loose horses cantering the wrong way round the cinder track met a television camera car coming in the other direction. The two horses took avoiding action by swerving onto the racecourse into the path of the oncoming field. It was sickening to watch, something you dread happening on any course when loose horses start galloping about unpredictably.

Richard has been booked to ride two horses for Dai Williams, Sonalto and Ketti. The ground is usually firm at Waregem but it has rained hard and continues raining hard through the day. Despite this, it does not dampen the Belgians' ardour for their big race. There are twenty-six runners in the Prix Jacques Du Roy, a two-mile seven-furlong handicap chase, a consolation race for those who didn't make it for the Grande Steeple, worth £13,617 to the winner. There's no prize like that in Britain until October. It'll be shoulder to shoulder like the start of the London Marathon and there's always a doubt in your mind whenever you ride on a foreign track lest you get hurt. But, at least, any crash landings will be into forgiving mud, not the normally bald concrete you get at Plumpton at this time of year.

They jump a practice fence on the way to the start. The previous year Carl Llewellyn had refused at it in front of a packed grandstand much to his embarrassment and consternation as he was about to face twenty-five obstacles five times more daunting than this brush hurdle. Roger Rowell, another British jockey riding in the race, mistakes Richard for a local and takes him to the wing of the first fence which is on a bend. 'Jesus, Roger, it's me,' screams Richard. Sonalto is brilliant at the bank, up three strides, down and off it. He's better than the French horses there and they are supposed to be '*au fait*' with such obstacles. He takes up the lead but with a circuit to go gallops headlong into a ditch, slipping in the combination of rain and deep ground. Richard rolls clear, his light waterproof breeches covered in grey mud.

It was with some apprehension that he was setting out for his next ride. Dai Williams had schooled Ketti himself and she had jumped scratchily. Richard took Ketti over the practice jump. There's no time like the present for a schooling session, so he jumps it twice. He regrets we don't have a similar system here though you couldn't jump a full-scale fence in cold blood. It would have to be the same size as a schooling fence. It would help get the horses warmed up.

In the race with horses around her, Ketti runs keen and jumps better than expected before ending up on the floor at the second last. It was a tired fall. In fourth place she just failed to help herself on landing, crumpling into the mud like an empty can underneath a foot. It is another easy fall for her muddy, wet jockey, the sort which doesn't even make you feel stiff the next morning.

The journey home was as eventful as the two rides. With his kit still wet and covered in mud customs went to town on taking apart his baggage, wondered what the white powdery substance (horse sweat) was on his foam pad and even took the end off his whip to see whether he could have put anything inside it. Then just to increase the tension on what was already an uneasy flight home, the plane, at full throttle, aborts take-off at the last second when a red light comes on in the cockpit. Some days it doesn't just rain, it pours.

September and there are another six winners to be chalked up. Progress is slow, the weight is a continual struggle until racing's gathered speed and held on a daily basis. In the middle of the month the Cheltenham and Three Counties raceclub invite him to join a panel of 'experts' offering hints and predictions for the current season. They probably regret asking Richard. He's not as co-operative as he might be. It is just one of those uninspiring evenings. He doesn't give too much away but when does he ever? Oliver Sherwood and Jamie Osborne, also on the panel, are more open and in better form but Richard has high hopes for Remittance Man again, no surprise there, Carobee, Another Coral, Waterloo Boy, Gambling Royal. Some potentially good horses, Wonder Man, Baydon Star and Mighty Mogul have just been sent to Nicholson's from Jenny Pitman by their owners Bill and Shirley Robins.

So far there have been a few highlights, a few moments. A four-day trip for Richard and Carol to Listowel, a sharp left-handed track, in Ireland to ride Four Trix in the Kerry National is one of them. On the way they cross a bridge underneath which children, up to their waists in the cold water of the river, shout, 'Throw me down something.' Carol is the type of girl who will rescue an injured rabbit and this is the green light for her. She insists Richard stops and then proceeds to throw coins for the gypsy children to dive after.

The grey Four Trix is not beaten far – less than ten lengths – but he travels well in the race. Richard rides Muir Station to win for Jim Bolger whose Irish Derby and King George winner St Jovite is shortly to contest the Arc de Triomphe. They stay with commentator Dessie Scahill, play golf at Ballybunion and take seaweed baths on the beach as there's no sauna. The idea is that you hire a cubicle, take a steaming hot bath, up to your neck in seaweed, then you're meant to gallop down the beach and into the Atlantic. Initially it leaves you feeling like a slug but it cleans the skin like no soap can.

The Irish racing authorities are more flexible than their British counterparts and it is demonstrated at Listowel. In Britain, if a fence is missed out for whatever reason during the course of a race, that race is declared void. At Listowel there was a pile-up at one fence in the mares' novices' chase and on the landing side an injured horse and rider are being attended to by medical and veterinary officers. The fence is blocked off, the remaining runners round it on the next circuit. No fuss, no bother. Here there's always a fuss, always bother.

During the course of a long season you will remember odd incidents and one such occurred one Sunday, as Richard and Carol made their way to Blenheim Horse Trials to give Scu, Steve Smith-Eccles and the remainder of the jump jockey team some moral support in a showjumping competition. On route a motorbike pulls out of a slip lane on to the A34 and straight into the fast lane without paying any attention to the Highway Code. The car in front of Richard's hits the bike from behind. The rider splats, spreadeagled, onto the windscreen before bouncing into the central reservation.

Richard, used to evading fallers, takes avoiding action, swerving onto the hard shoulder while the motorbike, as if under an inspired ride by the Invisible Man, goes solo for a furlong down the road before taking off up the embankment. Expecting to see a body more tangled than the motorbike and ready to dial 999 on the mobile phone, Richard and Carol are astonished to see its owner get up, shake himself down without a bother on him and wander off in search of his, now buckled, wheels. A stuntman on a carefully choreographed film-set couldn't have executed a more spectacular stunt and survived. The showjumping is an anti-climax after that.

Victory Anthem gives Richard his first 'serious' fall of the season in a novices' chase. When I say 'serious' it would probably have been a death blow by our standards and 'rubberman' feels this one all right. It's the gelding's first chase, his first outing of the season. It's all too exciting, like a toddler's first trip to the zoo, things happen too quickly for the excited six-year-old. For Victory Anthem it is not a race over two circuits, it's a race to the first fence, last one there's a cissy. He has not been the living best at schooling at home but he has had plenty of it. Two strides out you can see trouble ahead. You hope the undercarriage will come up in time. A stride out and it's too late to do anything about it. There's no response from Victory Anthem, there's a sickening thud, the clink of the stainless steel bit hitting the horse's knee, a rush of air. You try and sit with it, there's no question of jumping ship when you know it's sinking. You just have to remain with it, you'd be amazed how they'll find another leg and recover. They don't want to fall any more than we don't want them to. But on this occasion there is no salvaging Victory Anthem's downward trajectory. The horse gets up and continues, confused, with the chase.

The following horses don't do it on purpose. They'll miss you if possible. At Stratford it wasn't possible and the hindleg of another runner connects with the Dunwoody shoulder. His friends call him the 'rubberman', he could bring down a steamroller and, God willing, he'd not only get up and walk away afterwards but ride in the next. It's sore and for a moment he ponders how many pieces his shoulder will be in when he moves it. It is sore. He rings Mary Bromily on the way home. He'll see her tomorrow, Sunday, he may even be persuaded to give Fontwell a miss on Monday, Exeter on Tuesday, and be back for Cheltenham's first meeting of the new season on Wednesday.

Autumn 1992 was wet by comparison to some of the Indian summers we've had lately. Just when we thought the greenhouse effect meant there was no need to bring the horses in until the end of July – it takes roughly twelve weeks to get them from paddock to race fitness – because the ground is always firm until Christmas, it proves us all wrong. We're enjoying perfect ground in September but it's a long and winding path to the Cheltenham Festival next March. There's no point wearing out our best horses before we get there.

Schooling in the fog at Jackdaw's Castle. Tom Jenks, the stable's amateur, rides the grey Tug of Gold, I ride Wonder Man. All this takes place under the auspices of the ghostly looking figure of David Nicholson.

'I think you'd better ride mine, Richard.' The Duke and myself discussing the week's runners at the breakfast table.

Lord Oaksey and myself 'marking the card' for the guests of Colin Smith's Ford Farm Racing hospitality unit on the first day of the Cheltenham Festival. On the premise that I suggested most of my own mounts would go close to winning, most of Colin's guests would have left that evening with empty pockets, proving beyond doubt that jockeys are the worst tipsters.

Robert Kington, my agent and the brother-in-law of 'rival' Peter Scudamore, on my left, father George Dunwoody on my right. On the steps of the weighing room at Cheltenham.

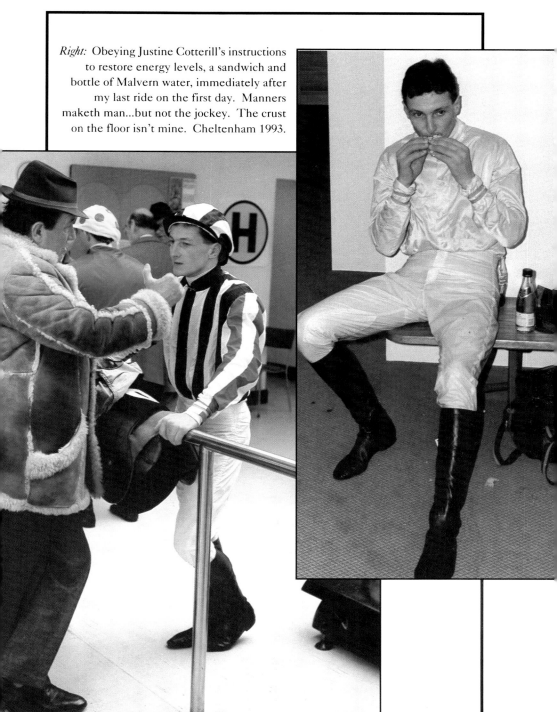

Right: Obeying Justine Cotterill's instructions to restore energy levels, a sandwich and bottle of Malvern water, immediately after my last ride on the first day. Manners maketh man...but not the jockey. The crust on the floor isn't mine. Cheltenham 1993.

Orders and instructions from the Duke after weighing out for Dreamer's Delight in the first race of the meeting, the Supreme Novices Hurdle. The sheepskin coat and barely visible red socks are the trainer's trade marks.

Shattered. It wasn't that bad a day, was it? Sitting at the same peg in the changing room as I did when Kribensis won the Champion Hurdle in 1990, his name is just visible between breeches and body protectors. Cheltenham 1993.

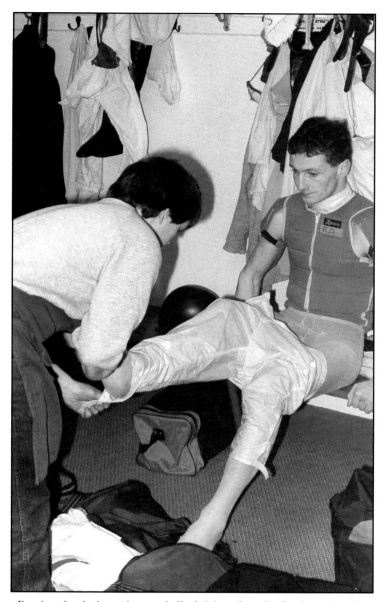

Proving that jockeys do wear ladies' tights after all. Getting a helping hand from Shane, one of John Buckingham's valet assistants. It also demonstrates how part of our armour, the body protector, fits. In the first race that day it had helped ensure I was able to ride again following Dreamer's Delight's fall. Cheltenham 1993.

A: Belstone Fox has stepped into the sixth fence. At this stage it looks like a one-way ticket and I'm in the brace position! Notice Belstone Fox's near-fore. It shows the strain on and flexiblity of a horse's joints and tendons.

B & C: Recovery in progress, a combination of both horse's and jockey's survival instincts coming into play. Horses don't like falling any more than we do. The expression on both our faces tells the story.

D: My sudden deceleration has left Andy Orkney on the grey Howe Street with problems of his own. Still, I'm sure he'd prefer this to being brought down.

Heading for home having jumped the last in the 1993 Tote Gold Cup. Jodami and Mark Dwyer have just hit the front. In the background is the famous Cleeve Hill while on the rails the female photographer, clearly neglecting her duty to snap the placed horses, is my wife, Carol.

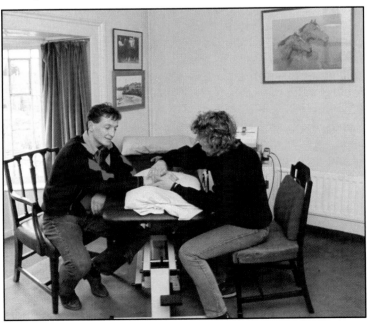

Rabbit Slattery, Mary Bromily's daughter, treating my injured hand. Northern Dancer looks on.

OCTOBER

Things start hotting up in October. It begins with that first Cheltenham meeting. Better horses are beginning to appear like shy badgers from their setts on a summer evening, tentatively leaving home one by one. You never know how much a novice might improve through the season after a summer at grass. Young Hustler, already having his fourth outing of the season, is the exception that proves the rule. He wins his second race in the Postlip Novices' Chase. He went on to win eight of his fifteen races including the Sun Alliance Chase. A couple of seasons ago his trainer Nigel Twiston-Davies was virtually unknown. His own progress has been as rapid as Young Hustler's.

There's no racing the following day but there is a Joint Riding Standards Committee at the Jockey Club Headquarters in Portman Sqaure. It is attended by Michael Caulfield, Peter Scudamore, Jamie Osborne, Graham McCourt and Richard who discuss the prevailing standards of riding with Peter Steveney, a stewards' secretary, and a number of stewards themselves including Sir Piers Bengough. Stewards' secretaries are the 'professional' stewards employed by the Jockey Club to look after local stewards at racemeetings and point out any rules that may have been transgressed. They have recruited Paul Barton, a former jockey, to their ranks in recent years, which has given more confidence in what they do. He is the poacher turned gamekeeper.

The Jockey Club show the jockeys videos of what they consider good riding and what they consider poor. They believe a good example of careless riding is Charlie Swan's finish on Cahervillahow in the 1991 Whitbread Gold Cup when he was placed second after beating Docklands Express. Richard never agreed with that decision at the time nor does he now. Though they proffer their opinions little comes out of the meeting other than a good lunch with the Jockey Club.

Autumn mornings are often spent schooling. For older horses and experienced handicappers this is just a reminder, for the novices it's a new subject to be learned. In light of a few fallers, not least of which was Victory Anthem's at Stratford, Richard helped persuade Nicky Henderson to stiffen his three schooling fences. Loosely packed schooling obstacles only encourage bad habits.

Trips to Ireland have been regular. Hop on a flight to Dublin, Shannon, even Cork and Bob's your uncle. Weekend trips to the United States are normally the prerogative of high-earning flat jockeys, the Pat Edderys, Steve Cauthens, Frankie Dettoris, taken there by their lucrative retainers, often on Concorde. Crossing the Atlantic from Wincanton is a logistically complicated manoeuvre. You can make it even more complicated if you want to ride in the 3.30 at Wincanton and catch the 6.30 to New York. It doesn't leave much to chance if the race is off late and the traffic's bad on the motorway. You've got no chance.

Philip's Woody, a horse named after Philip Barnard who was tragically killed in a fall on this track eighteen months earlier, is the reason Richard wants to stay for the 3.30. He has a favourite's chance having finished second in a bumper on his only start the previous season. He hits the front at the second last, hits the deck at the last. Now the action starts.

Richard is up and running back to the changing room not only before the St John Ambulance man reaches him but he's upsides, and holding his own, with the tail-enders. He even beat a couple. He reports in to the doctor, dives into the shower, doesn't bother with his tie as he rushes out to a waiting taxi who delivers him with screeching wheels to a local airfield like a carefully executed prison escape. A light plane, engine running on the tarmac, gets him as far as White Waltham, about fifteen minutes from Heathrow. Another taxi delivers him to Terminal 4.

JFK, New York, is a busy, bustling airport. If you didn't know it was in America you'd think it was Babel in Old Testament times after the language mix-up, certainly not a place where English was the main spoken means of communication. It is distinctly foreign, could be Colombia, anywhere south of the Panama Canal, you'd think. The cab driver sent to pick Richard up from the Long Island Chequered Cab Co. had presumably climbed out of bed the wrong side that morning and things had only gone progressively worse for him. An Italian-American he was in a foul mood, he was stressed out and had derived much job unsatisfaction during the day.

Richard arrives, a suitcase and holdall, and is rudely told to throw his own baggage in the boot. After a six-hour flight, it may be 9 p.m. in New York but it's 2 a.m. at home after a busy day and it has been hard to sleep on the plane. He is a humble, down-to-earth sportstar quite prepared to put his own baggage in the boot. There are no airs and graces about this would-be champion but he had, nonetheless, anticipated a welcome hand. Another cabbie meanwhile, a Puerto Rican, pulls up partially blocking Richard's cab in. This is the straw that breaks the back of the fragile tempered Long Island Chequered Cabbie.

Thus stirred to leave his seat behind the steering wheel for the first time, without warning he punches the other cabbie, picks up Richard's suitcase – it has never been the same since – and uses it as a weapon. An Ulsterman in New York. Bemused and slightly embarrassed Richard, whose arrival had precipitated the fight, watches the ensuing brawl as other cabbies try to separate the two protagonists. Wow, it's breathtaking stuff, a punch here, thump there, a flying suitcase. It is an eventful start to the Breeders' Cup Chase. His cabbie does not utter a word between the airport and the Marriot Hotel, twenty-five minutes from Belmont racecourse.

On Friday, 9 October he is to partner New York Rainbow for Jonathon Sheppard in a valuable novices' chase. He was trained by Nicky Henderson the previous season and Richard had won a couple of decent hurdles on him before finishing fourth behind Flown in the Supreme Novices' Hurdle at Cheltenham. However, before he is allowed to ride he must obtain a jockey's licence from the track office in the morning. It is a lengthy process involving a full medical, eye test, pee samples, fingerprints. It costs $120. He's made to feel at home, there are a number of Irishmen already there, Enda Bolger, John Queally who'd brought Cock Cockburn over, Donal Kinsella, his owner, Ciaran McKew, Charlie Swan – this is like going to ride at Bellewstown – and from Britain Richard Pitman, Jamie Osborne and Oliver Sherwood who had brought Young Pokey, the previous season's Arkle winner. Belmont is a lovely track, perhaps not the quaint rural charm of Worcester or Exeter, but huge practical grandstands overlooking the well-kept left-handed course and giant electric number boards. All American tracks are left handed which begs the question of what they do with horses that prefer going right. The facilities for jockeys are twenty-first century compared with Worcester or Exeter. Once a jockey arrives at the track in America he is confined to the changing room to prevent him discussing horses with punters. Consequently if a jockey is to spend three hours in there before he rides a certain amount of entertainment is required to prevent him becoming bored. At Belmont there's a large sitting room-sized sauna with a perspex front so you can sit and sweat – in front of the television. Half the trouble with a sauna is the mindboggling boredom so by placing a television within sight it automatically makes it easier. There's also a steam room, hot and cold water tubs, a masseur's room and a table for playing pool.

In the morning Jamie schools Young Pokey in preparation for the Breeders' Cup Chase, Cock Cockburn had been schooled by his lass Margaret with her raven hair, wonderful Irish sense of humour and bottle-top glasses. Only the French horse jumps moderately. In the afternoon New York Rainbow, always a careful jumper in England, is too deliberate over Belmont's point-to-point sized fences and runs a disappointing race. In the evening the British contingent retires to Nancy's, a local bar and restaurant which subsequently becomes the touring party's unofficial headquarters, for a drink and a meal.

Besides the Breeders' Cup Chase at Belmont that Saturday there were some major trials there for the Breeders' Cup, the end of season competition for the cream of the world's flat horses, to be run at Gulfstream Park, Florida at the end of the month. There was therefore plenty of interest in the meeting besides the big chase.

Richard had won the Breeders' Cup Chase in 1989 on Highland Bud. Since then the gelding, who in England as a four-year-old was second in the 1989 Triumph Hurdle, had sustained a leg injury and been given a year off. His owner Mrs Henley had died in the spring and now he was running in her husband's name. Like New York Rainbow he is trained by Jonathon Sheppard, an Englishman, who has dominated jump racing in the United States for years.

In the paddock Highland Bud looked a little burly and Richard cannot give him more than an each-way chance. He had been asked to ride Cock Cockburn in the race and he was wondering about the wisdom of having remained loyal to Highland Bud. The race is run over two miles five furlongs, sixteen fences, and heavy rain had altered the going from hard to good to firm. There are ten runners. Young Pokey makes a bad mistake early on. It is later revealed that he had strained his back with this awkward jump and it effectively puts him out of the race. Cock Cockburn, ridden by Charlie Swan, made a mistake upsides Highland Bud, and is another beaten early.

You couldn't ask for a better jumper of these fences than Highland Bud. Indeed down the back stretch for the last time he is going so well Richard is able to sit motionless and give him a long breather just in behind the leaders. Approaching the last he is still cruising. Then a gap opens between the two front runners between which Richard drives Highland Bud. The winning margin over Jonathon's second string, Mistico, is three lengths with the French trained Sassello a further three lengths away in third.

In 1989 there had been a nervous postscript to Highland Bud's victory at Far Hills, a country track. Richard had hemmed Ronnie Beggan in and there had been contact between their two horses at the fourth last. Ronnie had objected to Highland Bud. Richard was genuinely worried, thinking he would lose it. He had ridden in a race here before and been disqualified from fourth for bumping another horse a long way out. He had not found out until he had read about it in the paper the next day. The American rules are a lot stricter than ours in Britain. No contact is allowed at any stage of the race and if there is, whether it is at the start, middle or near the finish it makes no difference. At Newton Abbot you bump someone at the start and it doesn't matter. I don't think anyone riding would want it to either but at Belmont it is a different story. In the race before Highland Bud's in 1989 a horse had actually been disqualified for bumping another at the start, it's no joke. And American enquiries are conducted by a telephone link to the changing room, each jockey giving his evidence, not like it is here when you get summoned and stand, hands behind your back, giving evidence as if in the dock of a magistrates court. Highland Bud, on that occasion, was deemed innocent and allowed to keep the race.

There was no such worry this time though there were other problems. A visiting jockey has to pay his valet 5 per cent of his 10 per cent of the prize-money before he clears off out of the country, perhaps never to be seen again. You can understand the valet wanting his money however honourable the departing jockey. The Breeders' Cup, the most valuable race Richard has won, is worth approximately £80,000 to the winner. Before he'd be allowed to leave the track he was going to have to find and present over £400 in dollars to his valet. It's not the sort of small change a jump jockey carries round on him in New York.

A cash dispenser on the course which accepted his credit card saved the day, a day which once again wound up in Nancy's although the Irish contingent headed off for down-town Manhattan. Sunday's sore heads are cured, hair-of-the-dog style, back at Nancy's before the flight home late that afternoon. Having taken a couple of sleeping pills, Richard is able to grab three hours sleep on the plane before arriving at Fontwell, on Monday.

The National Hunt season is really beginning to step up a gear in mid-October. It's then back to Cheltenham on the Wednesday. Autumn racing there is round a new, sharper course called the Park Course but it rides well and Cheltenham is Cheltenham after all, the home of National Hunt racing. Another Coral finishes second to Tipping Tim after Distillation, a half-brother to Brown Windsor, has given Richard his first winner of the season at the course.

In Ireland Richard rides Montelado at Limerick to his first success over hurdles, the highlight of four rides there. Despite a run on the flat a few days before, Montelado is still stuffy and Richard predicts further improvement, the gelding clearly has a bright future. Keeping the ride on him for Pat Flynn is going to cause problems with Richard's own joint retainers with David Nicholson and Nicky Henderson. Before the deal this season he rode for Nicholson first, Henderson second (since 1989/90), with a clause allowing him to ride Desert Orchid when required. This had worked out reasonably well until the 1992 Cheltenham Festival when he had missed out on Remittance Man's Queen Mother Chase. The new deal was, in effect, a joint retainer. Where they clashed Richard would pick whichever he thought had the best prospect and in such instances he would go back and forth between both trainers sorting out something agreeable for both parties. Obviously there would be occasions when he got it wrong but it gave him more scope. There was one incident when he was at Galway after a newspaper had mistakenly reported that Nicholson had first claim. Believing what he read to be true Henderson was not at all pleased and Richard had nearly lost the job before the season had started.

Financially the old-fashioned lump-sum retainer is out and the incentive-retainer is in. This is where the retained jockey receives an extra percentage of a horse's winnings. Not only does it theoretically give an extra financial incentive to ride winners but, should

Richard ride a Nicholson horse to beat a Henderson horse, then the Henderson owner is not paying a retainer to the jockey who has just beaten him. It is common sense.

Back in England the better horses are coming out for their first runs of the season and Nicholson moves from Condicote to Jackdaw's Castle, a new purpose-built yard. Condicote had a sense of history about it, a cosy warmth about its nooks and crannies but in comparison to the well-planned Jackdaw's Castle it was something of a dinosaur. Baydon Star, a half-brother to the Grand National winner Rubstic and Kildimo, wins a handicap hurdle at Ascot, his first race since moving from Jenny Pitman to Nicholson.

At Chepstow, flat jockeys Michael Hills, Frankie Dettori, George Duffield and Ray Cochrane amongst others take on the jump jockeys in a challenge over hurdles in an event to raise money for the injured Nigel Coleman. It may be a gimmick but it is undoubted fun for all, especially the jump jockeys who could see their flat counterparts were clearly on the edgy side beforehand. Richard disputed the lead with Frankie Dettori for some way, coaching the irrepressible flat jockey at the same time. 'Sit back Frankie or you'll go over his head, now get your legs out in front of you.' Michael Hills, a regular in the hunting field, wins the race, Frankie finishes fourth, Richard some way back on Tomahawk. Mark Dwyer was the only faller – on Victory Anthem. There was meant to be a return match over five furlongs on the flat but it never materialized.

A couple of days later Remittance Man wins first time out at Wincanton beating Kings Fountain, a decent enough horse on his day, twelve lengths in the Desert Orchid Chase. It was not Remittance Man's most fluent effort. He dived through the third last and hit it hard. It is uncharacteristic, perhaps just rustiness after a long summer's rest. But otherwise it is a satisfactory start to the campaign for the previous season's champion two-mile chaser. At Newbury, on Friday, a meeting sandwiched between two days of flat racing, Travado and Mighty Mogul both win. Travado, a very useful novice hurdler the season before, appeared to adapt to fences well and Newbury boasts some of the biggest fences outside of Aintree. He had schooled quite quickly leaving little margin for error so you'd have to be pleased with the end result. Mighty Mogul carried 11st 8lb to victory in a handicap hurdle. You'd also have to be pretty pleased with that. Though Richard's day racing at Newbury is over, with two winners from four rides, the remaining race, the bumper, is cancelled when a light plane fails to negotiate the running rail on take-off and skids to a halt on the course. No-one is hurt and the race can be run at another meeting but the equipment to clear the course is not going to get there in time to save the day.

Saturday is at Worcester. Barton Bank beats Forest Sun easily on his chasing début in the Fred Rimell Memorial Novices' Chase. Out to supper that night and then to Galway for two days, two more winners on Sunday and Monday. Richard is at his brilliant best on Logical Fun, a hurdler who is never travelling well in the race but ghosts up the inside at the last flight to win a short-head. It is that close even the photo finish takes twenty minutes to develop.

October is not all winners though. As the tempo of the season quickens we have less time to ourselves, the highs begin getting beyond base camp, the lows plummet an extra fathom to deeper depths. Briery Hill is the first horse of the season killed under Richard in a race. Sure, you ride 740 horses in a year and you're bound to be on a few of the unlucky few. Briery Hill's life comes to a premature end, aged six, at the third fence in the Action Research Novices' Chase at Fontwell. The third in the three and a quarter mile chase is the second fence down the hill. Sometimes horses get too much on their forehand jumping downhill. Briery Hill gets too low and breaks his back in the fall. Horses can have spectacular falls and get up and gallop away but not Briery Hill. Jockeys have to steel themselves for such occasions, they become hardened to it. They mind, of course they do. They put on a brave face bringing back the empty bridle to the changing room. Then out of sight, these hard men who will go out and defy the doctor, ride with broken bones, often breakdown like children whose pet dog has just died. But it's the lads and lasses, the trainers who suffer, they know the horses the best, it is they who will miss not feeding Briery Hill the next morning, miss the character that tries to bite them as they enter the box, whinnies for his grub in the morning.

CHAPTER FIVE

NOVEMBER

THE LEAVES HAVE STARTED falling. The year is getting on, frail with its impending old age. November's here and for Richard it provides the most productive month of his career, thirty-two winners in Britain, two more in Ireland.

Chepstow, on the Welsh side of the Severn Bridge and where the flat versus jump jockeys challenge was held, is a left-handed, undulating stiff track. Unknown to most racegoers it sits atop one of the most elaborate cave systems in Wales. It is often soft because of its west coastal position. The championship, delicately poised that morning a week into the month, is 35–34 in Scudamore's favour. We were getting used to the jockeys' championship being all but over by November but significantly Scu had only had three winners in the last fortnight, Martin Pipe had had an uncharacteristically slow start, while Richard has been averaging nearly a winner a day. It is soft underfoot and an overcast day. Richard's first ride is Freeline Finishing with 10st in the second race, the South Wales Handicap

Chase. With five rides during the afternoon he doesn't want to push it. He no longer rides out on Saturday mornings, usually the busiest day of the week as far as rides are concerned, but nevertheless was up early to have a hot bath. He then loses another 2lbs in the sauna at the races, a very small, dark box where three's a crowd but it is good for sweating. He looks through the paper, could have a good day he thinks to himself if everything goes right. How rare that is.

He'll ride at 10st 1lb (1lb overweight) on Freeline Finishing. Had it been the last race after four or five rides he'd have been a couple of pounds lighter. To achieve that weight he needs to be 4lbs lighter – 9st 11lb – stripped. Jockeys are given 1lb at scale as an allowance for mandatory body protectors. A small saddle, light girths, light almost transparent breeches, silks, boots and body protector will come to about 5lb but jockeys get fussy when doing their lightest. 'Eh, John,' they say to John Buckingham, their valet, 'got a lighter pair of tights?'

Freeline Finishing likes the ups and downs of Chepstow, he won two novice chases there the previous season, and despite sharing favouritism with the brilliant but quirky Deep Sensation, he beats him two lengths having sealed it at the last with a great leap. Mighty Mogul is stepping up a grade in the next, the Tote Silver Trophy, a handicap hurdle over two and a half miles. He canters into the lead at the fourth last with his opposition struggling to go the pace and, despite only winning four lengths, the victory serves warning of what the future might hold. Mighty Mogul is beginning to make a big impression as a hurdler.

Richard wins the next on Shahdjat for Kim Bailey, a small chestnut mare who normally doesn't jump well but she does this time to win well over the three-mile trip. That's the treble up.

His last two rides are both favourites. You wouldn't think leading jockeys, the Scus, Dunwoodys, Dwyers, need confidence but a treble just gives them the edge over everyone else, they start seeing strides a long way out, their horses take a length out of the field at each obstacle, they're not panicked into rushing their mounts and gaps appear in impenetrable walls of other horses. Travelling Wrong is a big, strong gelding. It is his first race in a British chase having been a decent point-to-pointer in Ireland the year before. He likes to bowl along, uninterrupted, in front and on his own. Despite making a gurgling noise he wins by one and a half lengths. Thumbs Up rounds the day off in the last, another comfortable success. Richard rode four in a day before, as an amateur and several times since, but never five. What is more, in three hours on a Saturday afternoon, the championship has taken on a new complexion.

The five-timer took Richard into the lead in the jockeys' championship for the first time since he had led Scu two seasons previously when a broken leg had temporarily held up the champion. By Saturday night, celebrated in The Ibex in Chaddleworth, the score is 39–35 in Richard's favour. Bookmakers are less impressed and he is still 3–1 for the title but the gauntlet had been thrown at Scu's feet.

November continues to go well, he's like the surfer who has found the best wave, the one that's going to bring you all the way in and up the beach. Now Your Talkin trots up at Woverhampton, Barton Bank wins by thirty lengths in the heavy ground at Worcester. The form looks good.

King of The Lot keeps the ball rolling at Cheltenham's first three-day autumn meeting. It begins with the Countryside day on Friday 13 November, the Mackeson is run on the Saturday and on Sunday there is the first Sunday's jump racing following Doncaster's highly successful precedent on the flat. Another Coral is a well-beaten second behind Tipping Tim in the Mackeson. He had won the race the previous season and put up another brave performance. Travado, who'd been so promising at Newbury on his début, is not so fluent today. He makes a bad mistake at the first, another at the fifth and is brought down by Ascot Lad at the seventh fence, the first ditch. As a rule if you travel directly behind another horse over an obstacle and it falls there is less chance of being brought down than there would be were you a yard either side of it. Horses usually fall one way or the other, to the right or to the left. Ascot Lad though never took off, giving Robert Bellamy a nasty fall. He lands close to the fence on the landing side. Travado sees the other horse go, panics and has nowhere to land. He ends up joining the heap.

The first Sunday of jump racing has an almost carnival atmosphere from the Bishop of Gloucester's blessing, a Shetland pony 'grand national' on the lawn in front of the grandstand and various bands to stewards in baseball caps emblazoned with 'Sunday Best'. There is no betting – it is still illegal on Sundays – but it has everything else including an international jockeys' challenge won by Irishman Brendan Sheridan. The concept of Sunday racing doesn't bother Richard. It would save flying to Ireland. Although he enjoys those trips, and as much as a change is as good as a rest, they are exhausting.

It is a wet day but in the principal race, the Coral Elite Hurdle, Morley Sreet, having his first hurdle race of the season, beats his brother Granville Again and Scu. Despite there only being four runners and it being run at a snail's pace early on, it develops into a great tactical battle between the two brothers. Morley Street settles in behind Granville and off the bend the pair sprint towards the line. Morley Street pings the last and wins by a length, the former champion back to near his best.

Ascot the following Friday is not so good and the surfer wobbles to retain his balance. Morley Street, making a quick reappearance in the Racecall Ascot Hurdle, is beaten a head by Muse who gets up in an exciting finish on the line. Muse, with the evidence of more racing, would go on to prove himself one of the top half dozen hurdlers in the country though at the time, just five days after such a thrilling contest at Cheltenham, this was considered something of a let-down. Billy Bathgate unseats Richard in the next and Go South refused to race after the fifth flight of hurdles. Go South, a winner of no less a flat race than the Cesarewitch two years before, is one very good reason why complacency can never come into this game. Richard may be in the process of riding thirty-two winners this month but for all Go South cares he might just as well have been Coco the clown. It is one of those days.

Aintree's first autumn meeting for twenty years is a great success. It used to be a regular feature in the calendar but it had skipped a generation of jump jockeys. It seems strange driving to Liverpool, a well-trodden pilgrims' route each April, on a wet November week-end. Now Your Talkin and Baydon Star notch up the double for Richard while Nicky Henderson's Thumbs Up is beaten by David Nicholson's Dreamer's Delight in the last. 'Told you so,' says the Duke afterwards. He'd said the same thing when Travado had been brought down the week before and his Belstone Fox had finished second. 'I told you so,' he says, finger pointing out of his sheepskin coat. But the real fun, the day's thrill, is riding round the famous Aintree fences in the Becher Chase on The Antartex. Run over three miles and three furlongs of the National course, they start with their backs to the Canal Turn. Valentine's is the first. The Antartex makes the running in the rain, leading the eventual winner Kildimo for much of the way, jumping impeccably. He'd won the John Hughes Chase six months earlier and relishes the challenge that the big green fences present to him. However, though the spirit was willing, the legs were tired up that long run in and he is caught for second by his stable companion Four Trix on the run in and fades into third. But what excitement jumping those fences. That one ride round Aintree, no matter that it's not first past the post, is worth any winner you'd care to mention this month.

The ups continue to get higher and the downs get deeper. Wonder Man wins his first chase at Wolverhampton. Doesn't beat much but is impressive. Remittance Man wins the Peterborough Chase at Huntingdon, again his jumping wasn't perfect and had Uncle Ernie not fallen at the last it might have been a very close thing. Richard was having to drive him along going to the last. Perhaps it's the sticky going at Huntingdon, but the performance asks more questions than it answers. Remittance Man is an athlete, he'd been only average over hurdles and had been a second-season novice. But over fences he'd become breathtaking. He is the nearest thing to a natural jumper Richard has ridden – from the first time he schooled, just a different class to anything else. In a race he was very straightforward, easy to place, brilliant at his obstacles and his only defeat in three seasons had been his first attempt over three miles in the King George. He'd won the previous season's Queen Mother Champion Chase over two miles at Cheltenham with Jamie Osborne, Richard being claimed to ride Waterloo Boy. For Remittance Man he had altered his contracts during the summer with Nicholson and Henderson, so that he'd be allowed to ride him when he wanted.

Two days later. Nicky Henderson is on the phone. Remittance Man. His worst fears had been confirmed by his vet, the horse had suffered a tendon strain and would need to be out for the rest of the season. It is very disappointing to all concerned from the trainer, jockey downwards. It is a major blow to racing, too, when one of its biggest attractions takes a year out. Nicky had feared the worst but gave it a day in the hope that it might have been an infection, a knock rather than a strain. You wonder where he might have done it, blame yourself for pushing him too hard maybe on going he wasn't liking. He had struggled, was that the reason?

A flexor-tendon strain, or 'leg' as it's called in racing, is one of the most common injuries a jumper suffers. *(See picture of Belstone Fox at Cheltenham.)* A strain of the flexor-tendon, which runs down the back of a horse's lower leg, is rarely career-stopping but it usually means a season resting. In Remittance Man's case he was hardly lame and it was detectable only by a slight inflammation and filling of the tendon. The best cure is time but this is often sped up by 'firing' the tendon, which by inflicting burn scars on it increases the blood supply and supposedly the recovery rate, by various injections into the tendon or by synthetic tendon implants.

Newbury's Hennessy meeting is usually considered the first major meeting of the year, the Hennessy Cognac Gold Cup itself the green light as it were in the grand prix whose chequered flag is Cheltenham and Liverpool. Richard doesn't win the Hennessy. That goes to Adrian Maguire, who is earning the sobriquet 'the next Jonjo O'Neill.' Shorter in the leg than Richard he injects his carefree enthusiasm into his horses. He gives Sibton Abbey a pulsating ride, inspires him to run faster than he ever has before, to beat Jodami. From an outsider's view Maguire's ride is the highlight but from this side of the fence the two-day meeting gives Richard's championship chances a boost when he records a treble each day.

Newbury is a particular favourite. It is about twenty-five minutes drive away, and when you drive 45,000 miles a year, that is a good enough reason to like anywhere. It is a big course. If you took a consensus of opinion amongst jump jockeys they'd probably say this was the biggest outside Aintree now. It is fair and yet demands respect from horses and jockeys and, of course, the bigger the obstacles the greater the thrill. It is also a stage for some of the best racing outside of Cheltenham and we'd all prefer to sing in the Albert Hall than busk in South Kensington Tube. Its new changing room is spacious, the sauna's large and the showers work – there's much to be said for the latter after a sauna and five rides. The meeting has a winter steeplechasing feel about it. Next season's Classic hopefuls are tucked away in winter quarters, the nights are drawing in, the clocks have been put back and the good chasers have all had an outing by now.

Major Bugler, Travelling Wrong and Parson's Green all win on Friday, Carrick Lanes runs a creditable second in the last. Thursday's trip to Nottingham had been spent negotiating with the Duke about riding Nicky Henderson's Parson's Green. The Duke, in bed unwell, wanted Richard for For The Grain who eventually finished second and Henderson had left his decision about running Parson's Green late. These decisions could be crucial in the championship if it gets close. 'That was getting me more buzzed up than the actual riding,' says Richard.

On Saturday Mighty Mogul wins the Gerry Feilden Hurdle. He beats Staunch Friend four lengths and there are several other Champion Hurdle prospects in the line up including Flown. In the morning the Duke and Richard had hatched a plan to beat Staunch Friend whom they thought might beat Mighty Mogul, proven over longer trips than this, for speed. Stretch Staunch Friend all the way up the long straight and stretch him they did, making stamina more important than acceleration. Nevertheless going to the last, Staunch Friend was still cantering at Mighty Mogul's heels. From the last though the plan clearly worked as Staunch Friend found little off the bridle. Nobody had dared mention 'Champion Hurdle' in Mighty Mogul's presence until now, too absurd a thought for a handicapper. But this rapid improvement is earning him much respect. David Nicholson is taking him up to the top, a grade at a time, building confidence from very solid foundations, not with one great leap. This victory was sweet though.

Tyrone Bridge won the next, the long-distance hurdle, in the stewards' room after Burgoyne, who had beaten him a neck, had carried him left after the last. To the public it was possibly a lucky decision though Richard had no doubt that he'd get the race. Gambling Royal runs a good race in the Hennessy just fading up the home straight to finish fifth. He's getting weight off those who finish in front of him with the exception of Sibton Abbey but the others include Jodami, The Fellow and Chatam, and it proves he's not far off the top league. More time and some further improvement and he'll nearly be there. The afternoon, now darkening, the huge crowd already beginning to trickle home, winds up with another victory. After Aintree where he picked the wrong one, he's back on Dreamer's Delight and in a thrilling finish with Texan Tycoon ridden by Jamie Osborne, he scrambles home by a neck. On a cold day such a finish warms the blood like cherry brandy. Those who stayed to see it are glad they did, it is worth the extra half-hour in the traffic queue leaving the course.

The previous Sunday, Richard had taken a day-trip to Ireland to school John Mulhern's Flashing Steel, a big long-striding gelding who had been very useful as a novice hurdler though he had disappointed at Cheltenham when carrying Irish hopes. He is owned by Charlie Haughey, the former Irish prime minister. He had schooled well and his chasing début at Fairyhouse this Sunday is impressive. This is another horse to look forward to riding though to be constantly available to ride him will require the combined skills of a diplomat and a juggler. However, good rides have a habit of falling by the wayside through injury or bugs, if you're not very careful you'll end up upsetting more people than you please.

DECEMBER

It had rained winners, water and more water. December began with waterlogging and abandonments. Still, gives you time to fill in your tax returns, catch up on office work. Scu has a secretary, Richard is his own, enlisting only the help of Robert Kington to book rides. A break also gives you a chance to recharge the batteries but, against that, it doesn't do the weight much good. It is vital if you're trying to keep the 11st frame at a constant 10st that you raceride, and sweat, every day.

At Sandown Wonder Man improves again winning the Henry VIII Novices' Chase by a distance. He didn't beat much – Billy Bathgate had been up to his old tricks again falling at the ninth – but he still looked very good. And the old favourite Waterloo Boy beat Deep Sensation two and a half lengths in the Tingle Creek Chase over two miles. Josh Gifford is still searching for Deep Sensation's optimum distance. Waterloo Boy is a chunky little horse, the professional's professional, fast and accurate at a fence. He's never been blessed with the natural scope of Remittance Man, if you want to go long on him you'd have to lengthen him up a long way out. A veteran of the Champion Chase he has rarely made a mistake round Cheltenham.

He's come a long way since being beaten in a novices' hurdle at Taunton. His five-year partnership with Richard has been an enduring one and when others have partnered him Waterloo Boy has not always welcomed the change.

Mighty Mogul returns to action at Haydock in the Waterloo Hurdle, a race for which he's scared off much of the opposition and is long odds on to win. The conditions of the race mean that he gives the three other runners only 2lb. Because of the wet ground and heavy patches the first fence in the straight is to be missed out in the steeplechases. However a course employee fails to remove the cones placed in front of the first hurdle in the straight which had been placed there to guide the chasers back on to the chase course and prevent them jumping the hurdle. Richard screams at Peter Niven on Ambuscade and Russell Garrity on Bollin William to pull up. It is a rule of racing that should any obstacle be 'unofficially' missed out like this then the race be declared void. There was confusion among the jockeys. They were only cantering in the deep going but continued, unsure whether they were meant to have jumped the hurdle or not. David Nicholson even appears on to the track at the winning post but he too was unclear until Philip Arkwright, clerk of the course, ran on to the track asking him to tell the jockeys to pull up. By this stage the four runners had set out on what should have been the last circuit. They had eventually gone nearly two miles before they could be flagged down and stopped by a Landrover. Clearly if Mighty Mogul had been pulled up the others weren't going to wait and find out if Richard was right or wrong. This would have been their one glorious chance of success. The Duke, as you would now have expected, took over the proceedings.

The race is restarted with the rogue cones removed. Mighty Mogul wins comfortably from Peter Niven's mount Ambuscade. Though they had been four miles and jumped fifteen hurdles instead of two and half miles and ten flights, it had not done the horses any harm. At the same time, however, it was a cock-up by the authorities which had not done racing's image much good. It is also Richard's 800th winner and of that number one of the more eventful.

Richard's winning roll continued in the next race. Neale Doughty had got off his old favourite, the Haydock specialist Twin Oaks to ride Pat's Jester in preparation for the King George. Twin Oaks loves the mud and loves the place. They always say if the National had been run at Haydock he'd have been the next Red Rum but the closest he came in the Grand National had been fifth in 1992 behind Party Politics. He beats Pat's Jester in the Tommy Whittle Chase to record his eighth course win though 'Doughts' was to have the last laugh on Boxing Day when Pat's Jester finished second to The Fellow in the King George.

On Friday it was back to Cheltenham, more Festival rehearsals. Beauchamp Grace, making her début over hurdles, won the three-year-old hurdle by a decisive six lengths. It was an encouraging start. Travelling Wrong won again, his third victory from as many starts, and Richard has yet to see another horse on him as he is yet to be headed. In the staying handicap chase he had the choice of two, the Duke's Duntree or Nicky's Windy Ways. He selected Windy Ways, Hywel Davies is given the leg up on Duntree. Both are having their first runs for some time, Duntree his first for two seasons and with Hywel's overweight 13lbs out of the handicap, while Windy Ways had only had one run the previous season. He thinks this and the fact that Windy Ways is in the handicap will give Nicky's horse the edge – after all two years off is a long time – but Windy Ways makes a bad mistake four out and is pulled up. Duntree, meanwhile, provides what must be one of Nicholson's finest training performances of the season running out a four-length winner from Givus A Buck. 'I told you so.'

On Saturday, Another Coral wins the Tripleprint, formerly the A.F. Budge Chase. In November A.F. Budge had gone into liquidation and Tripleprint had come to the rescue by stepping into the sponsor's shoes. Another Coral is owned by Peter Deeley who owns Waterloo Boy; the two horses had been bought out of the same field in Ireland as foals by Anthony Stroud, now Sheikh Mohammed's racing manager. It is the highlight of another treble. Fortunately there is no band playing on this occasion. Another Coral hates live music and the last time they'd played when he was running he ran appallingly. Barton Bank had initiated a good day in the first place by beating Young Hustler on what was his third start and third victory. Shamana rounds the day off by winning the two mile handicap chase. It had been a busy day though, Dreamer's Delight and Morley Street had both been placed and Richard's other mount, Welshman, had weakened turning into the straight. Six mudsplattering rides in seven races. Only once does he get the opportunity to sit down for five minutes on anything other than a racing saddle. Only once does his cup of tea have time to settle before being drunk, only once does he have time to take a deep breath and actually think about what's already happened, what's about to happen.

Christmas is drawing near now. At Ascot, the last major meeting before the break, Baydon Star wins the HHS Hire Shops Hurdle comfortably to retain his unbeaten run but Tyrone Bridge proves very hard work, a test for even the fittest, and Gambling Royal makes a mistake early on in the SGB Chase, unseating Richard though it is a bad mistake. Normally when a jockey is unseated he curses himself for falling off when he feels he should have sat tighter. On this occasion Richard is satisfied that few would have sat on Gambling Royal's mistake. But he made the effort, Gambling Royal's cut mouth, where his partner has tried to pick his head off the floor and keep him on his feet, is evidence of the effort that went into the rescue mission.

Traditionally most yards of any size hold a Christmas party, much like offices do. Christmas Day 1992 is on a Friday and after Lingfield on the previous Monday there is no racing until Boxing Day on the Saturday, a five-day break. We're at the halfway stage, a good time to assess the progress. A cocktail of good fortune, ambition and singlemindedness combined with a very high work rate has taken Richard nineteen winners clear in the championship with seventy-nine winners against Scu's sixty. Even David Nicholson, who has supplied thirty-four of Richard's winners, is hustling Martin Pipe in the trainers' championship and is only £20,000 behind him, one decent race, in prize-money. The Jackdaw's Castle party is on Monday night, Henrietta Knight's on Tuesday and on Wednesday Sarah Bosley, wife of fellow jockey Martin Bosley, has organized the Jockeys' Christmas Dance in a marquee at a garden centre near Witney. It is attended by jockeys from the four corners of Britain and a chance for everyone to let their hair down. Most end up letting the side down as well. Christmas Eve is spent recovering and shopping in Oxford, a few friends gather for dinner at La Fontana, an Italian restaurant near Wantage, and return to Hyperion House for a drink. Martin Bosley does a good impression of Freddie Mercury every

Christmas Eve and this is no exception. Strumming a broom handle Hyperion House hosts a 'tribute to Freddie'.

Christmas Day is spent quietly with Carol, sister Gail and George and Gillian Dunwoody at Clanfield. Richard feasts himself on a slice of turkey, a few vegetables and a spoonful of Christmas pudding. It is the first time in years that he has had to do as light as 10st on Boxing Day.

Boxing Day at Kempton had become, in racing terms, Desert Orchid day. There's always a big crowd at the Sunbury course, just outside London, the day after Christmas, a chance for many to get out of the house and away from the turkey. In the last few years Desert Orchid's performances in the King George VI Chase had elevated him from mere racehorse to superhorse status and upwards on to superstar, far bigger than racing, far bigger than any human involved with the sport with perhaps the exception of Lester Piggott. If you could have asked him which his favourite racecourse was he would have said Kempton, spiritual home, scene of some of his greatest moments and now home to a life-size statue. The older generation of racegoers would never have Arkle displaced as the greatest chaser of all time but Desert Orchid – his bold, front-running style of running, his never-say-die courage, his unmistakable almost white colour, and the fact that he never took time out for injury – captured the imagination of the younger generation and mass media in a way only Arkle and possibly Red Rum had neared before. His presence was to guarantee large crowds of people from all walks of life who had never been touched in such a way by racing before.

He had originally been ridden by Colin Brown, he of the Ibex fame – we've been in the Desert Orchid bar before – and then Simon Sherwood whose nine victories from ten rides on the grey earned him a fame far beyond the betting-shop foyers of Britain. Simon had retired in May 1989 after riding Desert Orchid to his most famous victory in a rainsplashed Gold Cup at Cheltenham. Richard had taken over the ride the following autumn and, following in Simon's boots, rode Desert Orchid to his last two King George VI victories, in 1989 and 1990. In 1991 the pair, Dessie trying to win his fifth King George, Richard his third, had fallen spectacularly at the third last fence when fading out of contention behind The Fellow. All eyes watched Desert Orchid rise to his feet. His reception as he passed the winning post, his reins hanging limply around his neck, equalled that of the winner. It had been a happy but sad occasion of moved and mixed emotions, one of those days when tears had mingled with the relief. Dessie had galloped safely into retirement.

'Kempton was made for Desert Orchid,' says Richard. 'An easy right-handed course. The best race he ever ran for me was when he won the Racing Post Chase there, a handicap, with top weight.' He was not an easy horse at home though as Richard found out when he went to school him over fences in their first getting-to-know-you session at Whitsbury where he was trained by David Elsworth. 'He was best left to David's headlad, Rodney Boult,' says Richard. 'He rode him out every day and would just ride him with his hands on the neck strap. However it had got to the stage when he was so used to Rodney that if anyone else rode him he knew something was up. Brendan Powell had warned me that if he was running a bit keen with someone, David Elsworth would step onto the all-weather gallop with his hand in his pocket as if to pull out some polo mints. The first time I rode him David could obviously see I was in some trouble and not doing a great job at holding him. He stepped nonchalantly out onto the gallop – like only David Elsworth would – hand in pocket, but hadn't appreciated quite how fast Dessie and myself were going. We only just missed mowing him down.

'When I first schooled him David said jump the five fences and continue on to the gallop and do a piece of work. That was fine. There was quite a crowd watching and he was such a show off that he was even stronger than usual. He was keen and not paying much attention to the fences standing about three strides off each fence. Otherwise it was all right. The second year I was to do the same thing only someone had parked a tractor where I was meant to get on to the gallop. It was a miracle that I managed to pull him up in time and miss the tractor. But every time I rode him at home I had visions of Salisbury Cathedral looming into the view over the hill and it was with some trepidation that I would drive down to Whitsbury for these sessions.

'The greatest reception we got together was in Ireland after winning the Irish National at Fairyhouse on Easter Monday in 1990. Security there is not quite what it is at Kempton or Cheltenham and even before he'd left the paddock the crowd had surged in and swarmed around him, pulling out handfuls of his tail and patting him on the backside.'

His fall in the King George was the result of an antique engine, no longer what it had been in the glory years. Old age had finally caught up with him like it does with all athletes and in some sad way he had fallen trying to do something the wear and tear of a lifetime in racing no longer allowed him to do. And yet, though he had fought one fight too many, he was still regarded as the great Desert Orchid. His fall in some way was better than defeat and he was not, like a world champion boxer who took on one fight too many, ever considered an ex-champion.

If the 1991 King George VI had been big decision time for Richard – his loyalty being tested by Desert Orchid and the young pretender to his crown, Remittance Man – then there was to be no such choice in 1992. Remittance Man was out through injury, a few other options had fallen by the wayside. However, since the weekend before Christmas he had been on standby for Josh Gifford's Deep Sensation, a horse he had met and beaten three times this season. Declan Murphy, the stable's first jockey, was expected to opt for their other runner Bradbury Star, the more guaranteed of the two to get the trip.

This Boxing Day was to seem a long way from Desert Orchid's Kempton. Firstly there was the weight which had put a damper on Christmas lunch. It required more time in the bath and in the sauna at the races. Richard had not ridden since Monday and it was particularly cold which increases the hunger. Seven meetings on Boxing Day had been abandoned allowing many colleagues the luxury of big lunches, second helpings of roast potatoes, brandy butter on their pudding, though doubtless they'd prefer to be riding than watching Kempton on television.

In the Feltham Novices' Chase, which Richard had won the previous year on Mutare, a horse which he thought a great deal about, he was travelling like the winner on Barton Bank when he fell heavily at the third-last fence. In both his victories so far, though clear cut, Barton Bank had jumped low and flat. Admittedly he was quick in the air but a spill at some stage had been on the cards and, as sod's law dictates, that happens when it matters most.

In the King George, Deep Sensation failed to get the three-mile trip. Though Richard had done his bit for Declan and gamesmanship by taking The Fellow and his French rider Adrian Kondrat wider round the last bend than they might have wished or thought necessary, it was to no avail. The French horse passed Pat's Jester and Neale Doughty, his decision to abandon Twin Oaks last time at Haydock in some way justified, at the last fence and won by six lengths to record his second success in the race.

In the two-and-a-half-mile novices' chase Bishops Island gallops into the sixth fence and falls. To round off a moderate day, David Baron's Top Javelin is beaten less than a length into third in the three-mile hurdle by Sayyure. Richard is 1lb overweight. They say, as a rule of thumb, 1lb is equivalent to one length but at the same time you are that much weaker. It is doubtful it cost him the race this time especially as Top Javelin proves a hard ride.

Sunday took Richard back to the Emerald Isle for Leopardstown. His five rides include Fissure Seal, Montelado and Second Schedual. Fissure Seal wins the qualifier for the American Express Hurdle which is run at Cheltenham in March. Harry de Bromhead, his trainer, has told Richard not to hit the front before the last and approaching it he is running away but once in front Fissure Seal pricks his ears and idles. He nevertheless wins by a cosy three-quarters of a length. Both Montelado and Second Schedual found one horse too good in Bayrouge and River Tarquin respectively. Interestingly all three were to go on to win at the Cheltenham Festival although not with Richard in the saddle.

On Monday it is back to Kempton – a better, more satisfying day in contrast to Saturday. Three of them, Wonder Man, For The Grain and Mighty Mogul, win. Both horses owned by Shirley Robins, Wonder Man and Mighty Mogul, take liberties at the last. Wonder Man banks the fence, birch flies in every direction but it somehow fails to stop his forward impetus and he still manages to beat Atlaal comfortably. Carol, who is now assisting racecourse photographer Mel Fordham, is standing by the obstacle on both occasions and was so surprised by the horses' mistakes that she missed any decent shots!

For The Grain's narrow victory over Calapaez in the Tripleprint Handicap Chase is, in Richard's words, the best ride he gave a horse all season. The eight-year-old was coming back under him from a mile out and he appeared beaten everywhere but on the line. Richard drives him, shouting, growling and changing his hands, with the occasional reminders behind the saddle. Richard had also had the choice of Nicky Henderson's Tinryland in the same race and when he and Hywel Davies take up the running at the second last it is just the extra incentive Richard needs for one final thrust on For The Grain who collars Calapaez and Tinryland on the line.

Mighty Mogul is now shaping into not only a Champion Hurdle prospect but his performance in the Christmas Hurdle confirms him as the ante-post favourite for the championship in March. In Richard's mind his performance in beating Flown five lengths is equal to that of Kribensis in the same race during his champion year. And but for his stepping at the last the margin would have been nearer ten lengths. High praise.

Richard's toing and froing across St George's Channel is daily at the moment like one of his neighbours in Sparsholt might commute to London. Kempton, Leopardstown, Kempton, Leopardstown although the second trip is more logistically fraught than most. Richard is retained to ride at Stratford but there is a chance it will be abandoned because of the continuing frost. Consequently he has arranged to ride Crowded House in the Bookmakers Hurdle in Ireland – should Stratford be abandoned. He's booked his flight from Birmingham, not far from Stratford. Had he set off for Stratford and then had to turn round for Heathrow the chances of arriving in time would be slim. So when, as predicted, Stratford succumbs to Jack Frost, Richard re-routes to Dublin. He arrives, having been assured at 8 a.m. that there was no problem with the weather, to find Leopardstown a victim of the frost but, with a greater degree of flexibility than the British, they intend to run the race the following day.

There are seven runners in the race including Richard's old mate Cock Cockburn whom he, inadvertently, nearly puts through the rail at the fifth flight where Crowded House jumps sharply left handed. Later in the race he manages to get boxed in which necessitates switching off the rails. It makes little difference to the result which sees him finish a head and four lengths behind Novello Allegro and Muir Station. Royal Gait finishes fourth and, as he passes Richard pulling up, he appears to have broken down. A few yards further on he staggers, collapses and dies from a heart attack. This is the death of a champion. It cuts much deeper than you'd think when they have a history like Royal Gait. He had helped establish James Fanshawe as a mainline trainer, won Graham McCourt a Champion Hurdle to add to his Gold Cup, and connections believed he had another in him. Before that he won a Royal Ascot Gold Cup on the flat, been disqualified by stewards in top hats and tails, been trained in Spain, France and England. Richard had schooled him in his early days as a hurdler, helped him over those all important first few flights round the Links in Newmarket, keenly watched by the tall Fanshawe. In a rapid, cruel, unfolding minute they'd seen their idol come off the bend cruising as if to win. He had changed down a gear, more effort for less speed, as if he needed the race. Then the power cut and he just faded away. A Eurocrat among horses. It might have happened on the gallops or in his stable but you just wish . . . if only racing had been cancelled.

CHAPTER SIX

JANUARY

THE NEW YEAR BEGAN with a bang, literally. Cheltenham's traditional New Year's Day meeting was cancelled so Richard headed for Windsor with seven booked rides. The first is the Queen Mother's Dalliston, trained for her by Nicky Henderson. He had shown promise finishing second on his first two outings but this time he is prominent until falling at the third. In the next, a handicap hurdle, My Key Silca trained by Chris Nash, son of the late Colin Nash who had supplied Richard with his first winners, breaks a blood vessel. This is an increasingly common symptom of a secondary infection following a virus or bug and you can usually tell when it happens. A horse will be going well and he suddenly, for no apparent reason, fades very rapidly, in strides. His jumping often gets sloppy. Outwardly many appear to have nose bleeds which can splatter their jockeys with blood but internally a part of their lungs fills with blood, thus cutting down the amount of oxygen available. It does not usually keep horses out of action for too long but once they have had it they are often prone to it.

Baydon Star is out for a fifth consecutive win of the season in the New Year's Day Hurdle, the big race of the day and often a useful Champion Hurdle trial. It is a thrilling race and from the second last there is nothing between Muse, Baydon Star and Lift And Load. At the finish Muse, who'd beaten Morley Street at Ascot, gets up to win by a length, thus proving that his earlier victory had been no fluke.

New Year's Day was not proving Richard's most memorable, indeed it never has been a lucky day for him. Besides being beaten on a few odds-on shots Mulloch Brae had injured him at Cheltenham one New Year's Day which nearly wiped him out for good. His neck ligament injury, though not sustained that day, had been compacted on another New Year's Day. His next ride this New Year's Day is on Winabuck whose efforts to prove himself a worse jumper than most were paying off. From six outings he had fallen twice, unseated his jockey twice but had, when he completed, won and been third. His ability to gallop was not in question, it was just negotiating obstacles that was proving a problem. Why ride him? well on this occasion it appeared the chances of winning outweighed those of an injured jockey. He is still in with a chance when he gives Richard a crashing fall at the second last. It is the mother of a fall, the one where your life passes before your eyes and you have the terrible, haunting sensation of your head ploughing through the turf – if you felt well enough afterwards you would look for the furrow you've just ploughed. It is made worse by the fact that the winner, Avonburn, treads all over him.

This is one he won't be getting up from too quickly. He lies still, stretched out, trying to catch his breath. A good kicking can be exhausting. There'd been no time to roll into a ball, it wasn't one of those falls, and if he had Avonburn would have unravelled him. He lies there motionless before life slowly returns. He sits up, slowly, slowly takes a deep breath, then another. He climbs to his feet, gets back down again, it is too quick, he's not ready for that yet. Try again, onto his knees he holds his head on his lap, undoes his helmet. Another deep breath, another final effort and he's up, his arm held by a St John volunteer. Very sore, he gingerly walks, aided, to the ambulance. He may be down but, by hell, he's not out.

He hurts around his lower back (Mary Bromily, his physio, later believes he fractured his coccyx in this fall) and is angry, determined, stubborn, obstinate and, lest you thought it but didn't dare say it, mad. There can only be so many miles on the clock and you wonder if in twenty-five years time his body will be twisted with arthritis, every movement of every day as painful as it is when Avonburn has just walked over you. The doctor tries to sign him off. No way. He has already missed a ride in the second last and he's going to ride Philip's Woody in the last whether the doctor likes it or not. He knows if he's signed off there's a good chance he won't be signed back on the following day at Newbury. He convinces the doctor that he's fine though he is walking like Max Wall.

Philip's Woody is, like his jockey, headstrong in certain situations. When, not to Richard's relief, the last race is cancelled as fog rapidly descends on the riverside course at Windsor, he takes Philip's Woody for a gallop round the track just to prove to himself he's all right. The horse pulls hard, very hard, but this is a sweet victory. He knows he'll be all right to ride tomorrow after a session with Mary Bromily and a good job too. Another Coral and Scrutineer provide him with a double and Travado is back on a winning track at the same course on Monday after his heavy fall at Cheltenham last time. All three are being aimed at the Festival.

It is about this time of year that the leading jockeys hope that racing might succumb to a freeze up. 'Hope' might be the wrong word but it would be a relief to take a short break, a week, a weekend away in Paris. In the past Richard has been to Tenerife and Vienna. From Boxing Day until the end of January, Richard has thirteen falls from a seasonal total of about thirty-eight, roughly one fall from every twenty rides. So in just over a month he has 33 per cent of his falls. No coincidence he believes. The falls are as much as anything due to the fact that he is mentally tired, he needs the break. It is something he discusses with Mary Bromily. How many other sportsmen put themselves through this routine? What is more he is not the only one. Adrian Maguire is also having a spate of falls. It also coincides with the soft ground in January when horses perhaps need more help than they might normally on better ground.

Nevertheless the season is still going well. The bad days are still being outnumbered by the good days, the falls outnumbered by the winners, and after Kadi's victory first time out in a four-year-old hurdle at Sandown, Richard still leads Scu eighty-nine winners to seventy-one. The last two weeks have seen him win ten races. The bruise around his coccyx may make him look like the human equivalent of a stationary blue-arse fly but it is less tender now and he is walking normally again.

Providing he's not flitting off to Ireland, Sundays are the day Richard goes through the runners for the week. He'll discuss at length with Nicholson the week's entries. Placing horses is one of the arts of training and David Nicholson consistently places his horses well. The good horses, after a while, place themselves. The big races are so planned and spaced that there are limited opportunities and when they crop up these opportunities have to be taken. The worry at this time of year is that bad weather will screw you up, ruin your plans for Cheltenham.

Mid-morning on Sunday and Richard has a fair idea of where he will be going the following week and around Nicholson's horses he will try to work in any runners Nicky Henderson might have. 'Sometimes,' he says, 'on a Sunday you can see there will be a clash on Thursday and the sooner I work out which I want to ride the better. The longer you leave it the more you'll upset someone. In seven out of ten cases one horse clearly has a better chance than another. The difficulty is when you have untried horses running for the first time. It is one thing guessing about how a flat horse will run over a certain trip because they are working over similar distances but place eight flights of hurdles in front of a horse and it complicates things. You can only get a rough idea at home of how well they will run. In Kadi's case the Duke persuaded me I should ride him, he was very convincing. The alternative was Nicky's Spectacular Dawn who finished sixth. With those that had run, though, I have usually worked out the ratings and it is often obvious which I should ride. On most occasions it is very hard to get away from basic form.'

Placing horses well relies to some extent on reliable feedback from the jockey. When Richard dismounts from a horse he will give the trainer the benefit of his opinion on a number of topics: jumping, the going and any preference the horse might have, the trip, too far or too short, any quirks that may have come to his attention, perhaps it doesn't like being in front or in a pack, how it is best ridden, how it might be improved, its wind and breathing. Two seasons before he had recommended that Waterloo Boy, at the time losing his form, have a soft-palate operation. He has since won seven races, six of them graded.

January, if not characterized by bad weather, is characterized by the appearance of the season's four-year-old hurdling stars, recruited to jumping from the flat. Many, after hard seasons on the level but good enough to have been pencilled in for the Triumph Hurdle at the Festival, have been given a rest during the first half of the season and then brought out again after Christmas.

Beauchamp Grace, a filly, had her first outing at Cheltenham in December which she won. She continues to progress and impress. At Warwick she wins her third race – by a distance. It is one of those lifetimes in a day though. Shamana finishes fourth. Beachy Head is also fourth. Then it is Duntree's turn to take centre stage again. He has yet to complete the course since his win first time out at Cheltenham but Nicholson exudes confidence. 'Will definitely win,' he says – such bold statements from the Duke are rare. At the sixth last, going well, Richard asks Duntree for a long one. It is a definite question, there's nothing half-hearted about the asking of it. The Duke has always maintained, ever since Charter Party used to win or fall, 'Be definite.' Duntree's courage and confidence desert him as he is about to take off. He puts down, doesn't take off and headbutts the fence although his impetus gets him through the birch to the landing side. Two horses gallop over Richard and a third, Peajade, from the same stable, is brought down. Again it takes a long time for the wounded rider to get to his feet. He's got to have broken something this time you think from the stands. And then you see him walk unaided from the ambulance and exchange words with his trainer. You wonder in amazement.

Nicholson is angry. Richard is fuming, you can see the anger, the physical and mental hurt, welling up behind his eyes. Nicholson lays the blame firmly with his jockey, insisting Duntree has no problem with his jumping. He doesn't even ask Richard if he is all right, normally he's the first to ask after his jockey's well-being. He even announces to the weighing room steps that he'll be looking elsewhere for a jockey next week. 'I agree I'd asked the horse a sizeable question but not the impossible,' says Richard. 'He could, at least, have tried to help himself out.'

In hindsight the only remotely amusing thing was that Duntree had brought down the guv'nor's other runner. That always annoys trainers. Their relationship is only partially restored when Persian

Sword and his battered jockey are comfortable winners of the next but the air is still not cleared. It is perhaps the lowest ebb of their seven-year association. Four days later Richard drives to Jackdaw's Castle for a schooling session but has a chat with the trainer. They have both been under pressure, this has been coming to a head for a while. Richard had wanted to ride Travado at Kempton the same day that the Duke had wanted him at Warwick. However reparation of the fence is complete long before breakfast.

Nevertheless, the month ends on a tragic note. Mighty Mogul has run five, won five this season. He's a firm favourite for the Champion Hurdle, any more improvement and he will almost certainly prove to be the best hurdler Richard has ridden. His final preparation race is to be in the Wyko Power Hurdle at Cheltenham on 30 January. He isn't moving fluently, not even to the start. He's not lame but just feels scratchier than usual. He sets off in the four-horse race in last and appears sluggish. He paddles awkwardly at the third last and Richard, concerned that something is amiss, pulls him up as soon as possible. The vets diagnose a fracture.

Further X-rays reveal that Mighty Mogul has fractured his carpal joint. He'll miss the Champion Hurdle for sure, and the rest of the season. Whether his career can be saved will depend upon Mighty Mogul, not the racehorse but the patient. Horses are not renowned for being good patients. You only have to see fit horses turning themselves inside out on a Monday morning after one day off to realize that keeping them still is not natural. You can't patch them up like you can someone who has just shattered a leg in a motorbike accident. You can't tell them to lie still for two months. It has been suggested by the anti-racing lobby that this is where the cruelty comes in. They say injured horses are put down because, even if they mend, they will cease to pay their way. It is not that, and by God they tried their damnedest to save Mighty Mogul. They even flew a vet in from America. Just to have him turned out in a paddock would have been good enough.

The following Friday the injured carpal joint is pinned. Six screws are inserted to stabilize the fracture. First signs are good, the liver chestnut with a white splash down his face recovers from the anaesthetic. Radiographs taken the following morning suggest the screws have done the job although the first forty-eight hours after such an operation are always critical. At Sandown the Mighty Mogul team win the last race with Winter Squall. For a moment the worry is put behind them until a call is put through to the weighing room for the Duke.

While Winter Squall was winning Mighty Mogul had suffered a multiple fracture of an adjacent bone due to stress. It was no good. The vets don't need to ring up and ask for permission to put someone else's horse out of its misery, they just do it to save the horse any further pain. The Duke, the Robins, Richard, they've been in racing long enough to take the rough with the smooth. You have to take these moments as well as you do the highs but it brings a lump to their throats. Richard will watch the videos, wonder just how good he might have been, try and forget about the races they would have won together. He might reflect briefly on where it might have happened, at what stage of the race, why he hadn't been striding out well.

Again though it's worse for the trainer and the yard. Richard can go out to a restaurant for supper, forget about it, change the subject. He doesn't wake up next to an empty stable and in a way his biggest problem will be sorting out another ride for the Champion Hurdle. It's pure conjecture but Mighty Mogul may have been the best horse the Duke ever trained, we'll never know. He might run Baydon Star in the race instead now but you don't and can't replace horses like Mighty Mogul. And to add insult to injury, Gambling Royal, the stables' intended Grand National runner, has also been ruled out for the rest of the season with a damaged suspensory ligament. It is just one of those days and that night the Duke's drink is a little stiffer than usual.

FEBRUARY

February's first week, despite the cloud hanging over it, has been busy. Richard clocks up a hundred winners for the season on Grey Hussar at Windsor. Scu, though, is making relentless progress in his quest for another title. By the weekend he is only five winners behind, 102–97. Martin Pipe has sent out seventeen winners in the last fortnight. Scu's a warm favourite to win back his title. Again Richard says he won't let the Championship bother him until

Anything's possible...a smile. Clerk of the scales Peter Sayer weighs
me out to ride Waterloo Boy in the Mumm Melling Chase at Aintree.
As you can see under the number a large weight-cloth full of lead is
necessary when riding at 11st 10lb.

Heading to the start of the Oddbins Hurdle at Aintree. Lorcan Wyer is
on grey Gymcrack Stardom and I'm on Child of the Mist. Judging by the
expressions on the horses' faces the conversation must have been fruity.

Looking a little undernourished in the sauna with locals at the Thistle Hotel, Haydock, on the eve of the Grand National. They are about to go out for a few beers, if only...

Trooping the colour. Carol and myself leaving the hotel for Aintree on Friday morning. Upsides is Jimmy Frost who won the 1989 Grand National on Little Polvier.

Inspecting The Chair, one of the most daunting of Aintree's fences. The width of the ditch is 6 ft which makes it wider that I am tall. The height of the fence is 5 ft 2 in. BBC technicians are placing a camera in the spruce for a 'shot that never was'.

Stalking horses. Flown and myself lead over the second last in the Martell Aintree Hurdle stalked by eventual winner Morley Street and Graham 'Brad' Bradley in the brown and white and Champion Hurdler Granville Again and Peter Scudamore in the blue.

Inspecting the first. Won't Be Gone Long and myself with upsides the National 'winner' Esha Ness and John White. John looks deep in silent prayer while Won't Be Gone Long is clearly far more interested in Gerry Cranham, the photographer, than he is in the obstacle in front of him.

Eight out of nine. Eight of the nine 'non-starters' in the 1993 Grand National canter back to the start from the Melling Road. Left to right they are Judy Davies on Formula One, Jamie Osborne on Latent Talent, Jonathon Lower on Chatam, myself, Lorcan Wyer on Kildimo, Brian Clifford on Tarquogan's Best, John Durkan on Royle Speedmaster and Graham McCourt on Roc de Prince. I am retrieving the starting tape. The missing man out of the picture just for the record is Russell Garrity who rode Nos Na Gaoithe. (Copyright © Empics)

Off to the trenches. Trench coat kindly donated by Robert Waley-Cohen, owner of Won't Be Gone Long. Awaiting the verdict on whether or not the Grand National would be restarted with just the nine of us. It wasn't something we were pushing for.

Every picture tells a tale. While I talk to trainer Nicky Henderson, Simon McNeill, who had just completed a lap and a half on Bonanza Boy, is about to add some 'bite' to his coffee. Aintree 1993.

Viking Flagship at full stretch. The first fence in the BMW Droheda Handicap Chase at Punchestown. On the far side is Francis Woods on Killiney Graduate.
(Copyright © Liam Healy)

Scu and myself at Ascot after he had signed off a wonderful career
with his 1,678 winner.

after Liverpool but it is less than convincing. The black moods, the frustration, the pressure is beginning to creep into his everyday life. The dog is told to take a hike more often, the door is slammed more regularly. 'Goodbye,' he says politely on the phone and when it's put down he curses the person on the other end. The answerphone is left switched on when he's at home.

Racing has always been his life but this season it is taking over, inexorably, like an unstoppable demon. He's bringing his work home with him, not just watching the evening's SIS showing and cursing his own mistakes. Even on a good day the workload still awaits his attention when he gets home. Even after a four-timer tomorrow has to be sorted out, the day after, rides at the weekend. The moods swing according to what an owner might say, what a trainer wants, what his agent is unable to organize. It sparks a chain reaction. Outwardly we have a would-be champion riding the crest of the wave. Inwardly we have, in February, someone so obsessive it is driving him to despair. Up at 6 a.m. to practise what he will spend the rest of the day competing at. What about a private life you ask? Well, exactly, what about it? There is none at this time of year. Back home, supper, hot bath, bed. Maybe Richard Phillips or Michael Caulfield will come round but apart from Saturday nights at a local restaurant, that is it.

The Grand National weights have been published, two months before we make our way up the M6 to Aintree. The Jockey Club have announced new whip rules and it's gone down a real wow with the jockeys, Richard included. As from the start of the following season any jockey hitting his horse more than five times from the second-last fence will face an enquiry and possibly a ban if he is deemed to have been excessive. 'It just brings the whole issue back into focus,' says Richard, conscious that public opinion has to be taken into account. 'You pander to the animal rights campaigners once. Next it will be the whip itself and jump racing will follow. Jockeys have been riding well under the present rules. We just need to ensure there is more education for the younger riders and more education for the public through the press.'

The Cheltenham Festival is not far off now, a month, not much more. During February most of Richard's mounts will have a last pre-Festival outing. Several bubbles will be burst as the better horses meet each other in the last recognized trials for their respective races. Morley Street, that same day that Mighty Mogul went to the training grounds in the sky, had been beaten out of sight behind Mole Board at Sandown, virtually pulled up after weakening like he had hit a stone wall at the second last. Even one of Scu's Gold Cup possibles, Rushing Wild, had been beaten that day in a three-horse race at 8–15. At Ascot, Wonder Man goes under in his first defeat in four runs, and Mutare, a horse Richard has real affection and admiration for, falls at the last fence as he had done on his previous outing. Mutare had won the Feltham Novices' Chase at Kempton the year before in a time only two seconds slower than The Fellow won the King George VI Chase an hour later. He had shown real class that day, a cruising speed that just galloped the others into the ground. He had clearly had problems this season but no-one could put their finger on what those problems were. He'd broken blood vessels, initially in the Stayer's Hurdle, and the problem stuck with him. He'd go from Rolls-Royce to Morris Marina on three cylinders in two strides. To the outside world it looked like he'd lost it but he still floated at home, oozed class up Mandown. Ascot's last must have been a fence too far. He'd gone going to it, you wouldn't know what part of the engine had folded, possibly the heart, possibly a haemorrhage or ruptured artery. He tried to jump but his legs had gone lead heavy on him, he tried to pick himself up on the landing side after a heavy fall and for a moment, as he wobbled to his feet, it looked like he'd be fine. The effort was too much though and he lunged forward losing his fragile grip on life. Too late to say goodbye to a friend that should have been winning Gold Cups. Richard walked away, head bowed, hollow-stomached. Two great horses, great friends, partners, gone in four days. He had had some falls himself but this was the worst moment of the season.

Belstone Fox, Travelling Wrong and Beauchamp Grace go some way to putting things right at Newbury two days later. Belstone Fox is now getting his act together and his comfortable win should book him a run at the Mildmay of Flete. The filly has now won all four starts over hurdles and is looking good for the Triumph Hurdle, though it is always a difficult race to win. A treble on Friday and good old Waterloo Boy on Saturday. He is taking on Katabatic, a former two-mile champion chaser, for the ninth time. Their duels have always proved highlights despite Katabatic having won seven of them against Waterloo Boy's one. In the Game Spirit Chase, though, Richard makes all the running on Waterloo Boy and decisively kicks for home a couple of strides before his great rival and, without recourse to the whip, he sticks his neck out and beats Katabatic a length in another thrilling finish.

In Ireland Flashing Steel is very impressive at Leopardstown, and back at Worcester, Thumbs Up, a most consistent novice hurdler, wins a novice hurdle. He is quite a character and has to be held up in his races, he cruises to the front like he'll win half the track but the moment you ask him to quicken he finds nothing and starts stopping with you. At Leicester, Viking Flagship, whose career as a chaser had begun with a fall, has continued to improve and wins his third race since that improbable beginning. His jumping is, on the whole, good but he will let himself down by making the occasional error. At Leicester it was at the last when he already has the race in the bag.

But it's a crazy day at Leicester. Two winners apiece for Richard and Scu and in the last the Duke runs a horse that, despite being a half-brother to the very top-class flat filly In The Groove, he thinks is very moderate. At home Stylus has showed nothing. He wants the lad who looks after it, Robert Massey, to ride it instead of Richard, just to give him a bit of fun as much as anything. Besides, at 150–1 in a five runner race the Duke wasn't the only one at Leicester who was thinking so. Anyway, to cut a long story short, Stylus bolts in, beating the second fifteen lengths. They'll kick themselves if Richard, who hears the result in muted disbelief on the car radio, is beaten by one in the championship.

CHAPTER SEVEN

MARCH

IT IS MONDAY, 8 March. 'Christ they're up early,' thinks Richard Dunwoody to himself as he speeds past a yellow sign, hurrying on towards Stow-on-the-Wold and ultimately to Jackdaw's Castle. The Duke wants to school his Cheltenham horses, just give them one last reminder. Richard is going too fast to notice the precise wording on the signs but there can only be one direction in which they point. Of course he knows the Festival is just around the corner but it is the little things, like the AA road signs, that just remind you of the impending Cheltenham Festival.

You think Christmas Eve was exciting as a child, waiting to unwrap surprises. This is going to be the same. There'll be surprises, maybe a couple of presents you hoped for, possibly a couple of presents you didn't really want. You've posted your letter to Father Christmas up the chimney. Passing those signs though, 'Cheltenham N.H. Festival traffic, via Stow', it is like opening another window in the advent calendar.

The previous day had been Richard's first day off for twenty-nine days; six days in England and on the Sabbath when it is decreed that the rest of us take the day off, it's an away day to Ireland. No need to be a clairvoyant to know that the next invitation had been accepted. Curious sporting magazines, on athletics, boxing, rugby league, are strewn around the sitting-room floor at Hyperion House. It means only one thing, it's *Question of Sport* time again. The perfectionist's perfectionist – the man who's rarely satisfied with his own performance – has his own standards to keep up. He wants to be able to recognize Gordon Brand Jr on the number board.

So this particular Sunday, in most of our eyes, is hardly a day off, except under the guise that a change is as good as a rest. Following Newbury races, he and Carol drive straight to Manchester for supper and afterwards a drink with Ian Botham and his wife. The quiz is filmed the next afternoon after a good lunch. The whole atmosphere is very relaxed. You get plenty of wine for lunch, Botham tells a few good stories, Beaumont chips in, David Coleman laughs at the other end of the lunch table. A comic warms up the crowd and after a couple of glasses of wine his jokes seem funny. Then, of course, you can take all day to answer a question. The editors will deal with it, make the end result snappy. Despite the presence of cameras the whole thing is horizontally laid back. If only Cheltenham were like that. John Reid is on first and falls early on when asked who had won the 1991 Derby. The answer is Generous but, John wonders, was it himself on Dr Devious! In the second sitting Richard teams up with Bill Beaumont and David Phillips, a Norwich footballer. The opposition, captained by Botham with Adrian Moorhouse the swimmer and Paul Hodgkinson, are well beaten.

Schooling sessions on a Monday when the horses are fresh can be hairy. They don't always concentrate after a day off. This particular morning is attended by Brough Scott, presenter of Channel Four Racing and award-winning journalist, and a photographer. Brough used to ride, he remembers these mornings, when things just don't quite go to plan.

Viking Flagship and Richard, upsides Strong Beau and Tom Jenks, lead Duntree and Carl Llewellyn up over the fences. There's a crash behind Richard but he's too intent on his own business to look over his shoulder. Only when he pulls up and is joined by a loose Duntree does he realize what has happened. Carl had been deposited at the lurking Scott's feet. That's good copy. The others, including Kribensis, who is lodging at Jackdaw's Castle until the Champion Hurdle, all jump well.

Next to the jumping paddock – an enclosed area – to school Barrica and The Flying Footman. With the bulk of the schooling finished and all the important horses out of the way, Richard can relax a little though he never drops his guard. No problems are anticipated with either horse. At the first both try to run out, at the second Barrica, something of a madam, attempts the same manoeuvre but Richard again keeps her in. This time, however, she stops. Urged on over by Richard from a standstill, she swings him round underneath her, trampling and then dragging him as he obstinately hangs on to the reins. Even better copy. The week before Cheltenham begins with an unwelcome addition to the season's collection of bruises. They are laughed off at breakfast.

A faller in the morning, a winner in the afternoon, is the old racing adage. This is the exception to the rule, Lady Luck fails to turn up at Wolverhampton that afternoon. One horse makes a noise which impairs its breathing. Another slithers to its belly over the water and the partnership is dissolved. Another, Visaga, breaks a blood vessel and Richard pulls it up. 'Over-rated bastard,' is the only printable abuse he gets from one disgruntled punter who had backed Visaga, the second favourite. We play to a fickle gallery at times.

A day's shopping in London on Tuesday is followed by a massage session with Val Ridgeway at Newbury on the way home. Legs, arms, back, neck, ribs, the lot. He didn't realize he was covered in so many bruises heading towards the most important week of the season.

Nicky Henderson schools his horses on Wednesday. Jamie Osborne partners Travado whom he will ride in the Arkle in which Richard has been booked for some time to ride Wonder Man. Jamie enjoys schooling at speed so Richard, who prefers more haste and less speed, just this once lets him have it. Travado and Whatever You Like, tracked by Acre Hill, rattle over the three fences like bats out of hell. Richard has rarely schooled faster but Jamie doesn't flinch.

With less than a week to go Richard and Robert Kington have sorted out most of his rides, the principals being Flown in the Champion,

Waterloo Boy in the Queen Mother Champion Chase and Another Coral in the Gold Cup. The only hiccup at the moment is that he has to ride Duntree in the Ritz Club Chase and he still has a choice in the Festival Bumper, a championship flat race for National Hunt horses over the age of four. You wouldn't mind riding Duntree in the last race on the last day of the Festival but in the Ritz on the first day? At this stage it is something to laugh about but to be honest you're looking to avoid the equivalent of a World Wrestling Federation body slam on day one. The trip to Folkestone is spent making the choice between Mick O'Toole's Diplomatic and Homer Scott's Rhythm Section in the Bumper. Both men are on and off the phone. It is a hard decision, both are very good salesmen and it is difficult to turn either down. No-one seems clear on which is the best, Richard rings several contacts in Ireland, including other trainers, pressmen and jockeys, to find out. Eventually he plumps for Diplomatic.

Thursday is another schooling morning. This time at Ian Balding's Kingsclere yard just below Watership Down. Jimmy Frost has been banned for the weekend and Richard will take over the ride on Spinning in the Imperial Cup at Sandown but he is a notoriously hard puller. Richard envisages an unscheduled tour of rabbit country but Spinning proves to be a gentleman and allows Richard the spectacular panoramic views from the downs across Berkshire after schooling over eight flights. Ian, who schools one of his point-to-pointers, is still stylish and still a good horseman despite being the wrong side of fifty. He hasn't lost it.

Living like you do, on the edge, other people's misfortune, to a point, is a continual source of amusement, as much as your own mishaps. Carl hitting the deck on Duntree, for example, provided much hilarity. Richard's own spill from Barrica caused much mirth. At Kingsclere after first lot the string is enjoying a pick of spring grass when one of the lads lets go a two-year-old which, with the saddle acting like a bucking-strap, goes bananas. For a few moments it is the trainer's nightmare but to everyone else it is the source of much amusement.

The spring is going to be coiled tight next week and, while aware of the Festival, Richard is trying to keep it from playing on his mind. Michael Caulfield comes round for supper that evening, he has just a week earlier ridden in his first race, a charity event at

Ludlow, and is still on a high. Michael has made the transition from raw novice to hardened professional very rapidly and is already talking about booking his rides for the Festival. 'Shall I give Pipey a ring?' he asks Richard. Something of jester in the King's court he is the ideal antithesis for Richard who, in conversation, prefers to be entertained than to entertain.

At Wincanton he keeps the pressure up on the Championship with a double. Scu, probably beaten anyway at the time, falls at the second last which allows Amtrak Express a comfortable victory in the Novices' Hurdle. Smartie Express, an old handicapper, gives him as good a ride as he'll get all season, makes most of the running and jumps from fence to fence. Even Barrica who runs averagely makes up for the pride-denting schooling session by jumping well in the novices' chase. On the way home with Graham McCourt they ring the Overnight Jockeys (OJOCS) to get the five-day entries for the first day of the Festival. Straightforward, twenty-two in the first in which Richard rides Dreamer's Delight. Montelado, the horse he would like to ride in it, is also entered. Second race, thirteen entered, Wonder Man, twenty-six in the Champion Hurdle.

On Saturday, by which time the first horse, Montelado, has already arrived at Cheltenham, Richard has hired a helicopter to fly him from Chepstow to Sandown, enabling him to ride both Winter Squall and Panto Prince in the 2.00 and 2.30 in Wales before arriving at the Esher track to ride Spinning in the 4.10. Though both horses win at Chepstow it is not a cheap exercise. The helicopter costs £869 and though it is divided between owners and Peter Hobbs, another jockey, it still costs Richard £400. The evening is spent at Liaison, a Chinese Restaurant in Oxford. Paul Barton, an ex-jockey and now a stipe (stewards' secretary), used to be a partner in it. Its Chinese proprietor, Timmy, is a gambling man. It is, if you like, a pre-Cheltenham evening out.

On Sunday he goes through all his rides with Robert Kington, the Duke and Nicky Henderson. Afterwards, late morning, there is one last respite before Cheltenham's grandstands loom into view round the side of Cleeve Hill. A boomerang, yet to be used since it fell out of its holly-decorated wrapper at Christmas, is just the toy to take his mind off the coming week. Its flight is as uncertain as the coming week's rides, only when the boomerang doesn't come to heel as it's supposed to, there is no obvious sign of frustration. From here on in the tension is going to be mounting, overbearing and exhausting.

THE CHELTENHAM FESTIVAL

The Cheltenham National Hunt Festival is a mecca for enthusiasts of the winter game. As a magnet is to iron, as Lourdes is to the incurably ill, as nectar is to bees, so Cheltenham is to the National Hunt fraternity. For owner, trainer, jockey, purist or part-timer, there is no better. When you start out in this game you long just for a ride there, perhaps, if you're an amateur, in the National Hunt Chase, in front of heaving, roaring stands, crowds of 40,000. Then you get more ambitious, you want to win there, anything, just to savour the walk back in front of the stands, past outstretched hands of congratulations, past cheering crowds, the focus of attention. Championships are one thing but for three days each spring, winning here is something greater.

Richard Dunwoody is here. It is not a surprise because we have established that he's tough but his one 'quiet' warm-up ride at Plumpton the previous day crashed through the third-last fence and for a split-second the names of Flown, Wonder Man, Waterloo Boy had flashed before his eyes like life does in moments of great danger. For the gladiators, though, a sling is a most unsatisfactory form of dress for the Festival. Make no mistake there are plenty in attendance unable to enter the fray, Brendan Powell nursing his second broken leg in two years, Richard Guest trying to break a recovery record in his attempt to be fit to ride Romany King in the Grand National, a fortnight and a few days hence, Mark Richards who had his knee cap amputated after being kicked at the start. These are the unlucky few, as determined to be back next season as their fit colleagues will be when they land in front over the last out there on the playing field in the afternoon.

The course at Cheltenham is undulating. Past the stands you swoop downhill to your left, down to the water, over the first of the ditches with their notoriously high orange and grey guard rails. Up another hill where races sort themselves out for the run down to the third-last fence or second-last hurdle. Here horses start racing, travelling faster than they have ever run before, magnifying mistakes and placing greater importance on the split-second decision of each jockey. Then it's up and round the home turn and into a roaring tunnel of noise and people, uphill all the way to the line.

Some horses don't like the undulations, don't like Cheltenham. Some are unsettled by the noise before they have even started. Others are caught out by the high guard rails that precede the ditches. Those are the bad falls, when your mount misjudges the guard rail. In a split second his head comes up then disappears underneath you. During this same split second he is decelerating from 30 mph to zero, while you, the human cannon ball, gain an extra 10 mph and hit the ground at about 40 mph. Though your horse doesn't always fall, staying on is an impossibility. It happened to Richard on Roadster a long time back.

Richard doesn't ride out during the Festival, there simply isn't the time. His first race of the day is to beat the traffic as racing folk descend on the Gloucestershire spa town. Rising at 7 a.m. is something of a lay-in. Sometimes during the meeting he doesn't sleep well, he's restless. It was when he rode Celtic Chief in the 1988 Champion Hurdle that he came close to losing his head. He always reflects on it, tries to avoid a repeat. It was his second ride in the race and the horse was favourite. He was so tense he had had to go for a run the evening before, running faster and further around the streets of Bampton where he was living at the time. 'I couldn't sleep, I tried the spare room, I couldn't sleep there either. I don't know whether it was the fact I was riding for Mercy Rimell! Or whether it was just the apprehension, the excitement, the expectancy.' Now he tries to keep to the same routine, gets up at seven, collects the papers, reads them, swots up form like a student's last-minute revision, reminds himself what the opposition are likely to do, what they are capable of accomplishing.

Richard's fitness for Cheltenham is taken for granted. With over 550 rides in Britain alone since the start of the season that has taken care of itself. At this stage a break of a couple of days would be more beneficial than a jog or session in the gym. Mentally he will ride each race several times in his own mind before actually getting to sit on his mount in the paddock. The process, an important part of Richard's job, is called visualization. He'll run through the various possibilities of what will happen, what he should do if he's left in front at a certain stage, who he shouldn't track, where in an ideal world he will be at a certain stage of the race. He will have done this homework the evening before, possibly watching the videos of a couple of races just to remind himself of a few points. The process may be repeated before breakfast, on the drive to the course. You may not get an answer when you ask him a question, his mind far away.

When he arrives there is already a buzz about the place despite it being the best part of three and half hours before the first race. Many people are already at the course and in the weighing room. Gatemen at the ready, gypsy women, a dirty brown, selling 'lucky' heather, with an ability to make you feel guilty for not forking out. Spiv-like touts operate 50 yards from the entrances with the subtlety of sledgehammers and as blatant as beggars. ' 'Ere mate, wanna buy a ticket?' one asks Richard despite a couple of saddles under his arm and a heavy kit bag in the other. Perhaps he's more at home outside Wembley – when Elton John is playing there. There never used to be that many around but now, by lunchtime on Tuesday, they've marked out their own territory like lions in the jungle, some working in pairs, others alone. Inside the course relaxed officials make last-minute checks and uniformed catering staff, some of the 2,000 employed over the three days, scamper from kitchen to marquee, marquee to kitchen. A salesman from Garrards, one of nearly seventy stalls in the tented village, polishes a necklace with the same attention to detail that lads will later give to the quarter marks on horses' backsides, the final touches. A groundsman puts the last hanging basket of flowers in place beside a tunnel underneath the stands which leads to the lawn. Spectators file in and head for lunch in the hospitality area below the paddock and helicopters begin purring into sight over Cleeve Hill like a scene from *Apocalypse Now*.

Outside the weighing room, Richard Pitman waits with a two-man crew from SIS. 'Can I grab you, Woody?' he asks. 'Just a brief word about Flown.' Snowy Lewis, the door attendant, greets Richard like a long-lost friend. He'll count them out and count them in for the next three days. 'Good luck today, Richard,' he says. He'll wish each and every jockey the same when they arrive. The clerk of the scales, Peter Sayer, is reading the *Racing Post* at his table. The starter,

Keith Brown, wanders in and hangs up his mackintosh in case it rains. Tim Holland-Martin and Nigel Clark, both acting stewards, stroll in and out of the stewards' room deep in discussion. Edward Gillespie, course manager, speaks to someone on the other side of the course through a walkie-talkie. Philip Arkwright returns from inspecting a part of the course.

A number of jockeys will have arrived at the course earlier than Richard. A few of the Irish who have come straight from the airport with their suitcases. John Buckingham takes his saddles and puts them up on his peg. 'I'll be getting changed early because I've a hospitality tent to do,' says Richard.

Already in the sauna are Mark Pitman, Hywel Davies, Peter Scudamore and Peter Niven. It's like being at the hairdressers for gossip. Mark, nicknamed Percy, unloads the more unsavoury details of his most recent private life, he has been up all night with a bug, thought the world had fallen out of his bottom, all the old jokes about diarrhoea. At one stage he had such a temperature he didn't think he would ride and he had to go to the doctor three times. Didn't think he'd need a sauna after it at any rate. Hywel has the verbal equivalent of Percy's ailment. He can turn a minor incident into a twenty-minute epic. He is just returning from injury and tells Richard how Uncle Mogy, one of the Duke's, had nearly killed him at Hereford. Hywel is the main subject of his own conversation. News then filters through with the entry of another jockey. 'Is it true about Dai Tegg?' asks Simon McNeill. 'He's apparently had a brain tumour and is critical in hospital.' Carl Llewellyn, who is to substitute for him on Flakey Dove in the Champion Hurdle, confirms the authenticity of the story. 'Yep, brain haemorrhage or something like that.' Percy is faintly embarrassed that he has been moaning about tummy ache when his colleague is in hospital in a critical condition, his life in the balance. Then a stewards' secretary pops his head round the sauna door. 'All the Irish jockeys are wanted by the stewards,' he says. It is to familiarize them with the whip rules. 'What's wrong with the Welsh?' retorts Hywel. 'And us Scottish?' adds Niven and the stewards' secretary leaves before he gets any more stick.

Richard, showered and changed, is in what we used to call standard dress at school, bottom half his uniform of breeches and boots, top half a smart jacket. He is to talk to Colin Smith's Ford Farm Racing, the company that runs Jackdaw's Castle. It gives him a chance to just go through the races once more, remind himself of the opposition. Public speaking is something sportsmen are required to do but an exercise in which they receive no formal training. A few like John Francome are naturals. Richard is not naturally talkative nor is he a stand-up comedian. Bold on a horse he may be, but bold in front of forty guests he is not. In some ways giving this talk is worse than riding. He's had plenty of practice now and is no longer the fish out of water he used to be but it has taken time to get to this stage and it is made easier as John Oaksey puts questions to him.

The feature of the first day is the Champion Hurdle, sponsored this particular year, for the third time, by the Jefferson Smurfit Group. It is run over two miles and half a furlong. The race is worth £120,000 of which the winning owner collects £63,125 and, as is now the custom with big races, the prize money extends to the sixth-placed horse. Richard won the race in 1990 on the grey gelding Kribensis, at the time a six-year-old, owned by Sheikh Mohammed and trained by Michael Stoute, better known as a flat trainer and for his successes with horses like Shergar and Shahrastani, better known for employing Walter Swinburn than Richard Dunwoody. Kribensis was again in the line up today, but his career in the three years since he had been crowned champion had been injury plagued and he was not considered a major threat now at the age of nine.

'He was a grand ride,' recalls Richard. 'He was not over big but all there. As racehorses go he was easy to ride, not at all complicated. He had been one of the few favourites ever to have won the Triumph Hurdle as a four-year-old. Steve Smith-Eccles who has a near monopoly on Newmarket jumpers had been due to ride him but was bound to partner Surf Board for Nicky Henderson that year and the Duke, a good friend of Anthony Stroud who is the Sheikh's racing manager and had bought Another Coral and Waterloo Boy out of a field, had helped me get the ride. In his slower paces he was a scratchy mover but he was always a good jumper from the word go, very professional, never too low although he could give the occasional flight a bit too much daylight. He was never over-raced and remained unbeaten until he ran in the 1989 Champion Hurdle. That year he had shared the lead over the last but in the softer ground he faded to finish ninth behind Beech Road whom Richard Guest had brought, unseen, up the standside rails.

'When he won the following year it somehow seemed very expected. Looking back it did not seem a hard ride but after the race I was tired. I had been very tensed up during the race because of the expectancy and because I know how often in racing the expected doesn't happen. The sensation of winning was as much a feeling of relief. Unlike the Gold Cup or National which are followed by amateur races there was little time to appreciate it and take it all in or dwell on it. I had to go out and ride Bluff Cove in the next following a television interview and, of course, there were still another two days of the Festival to go, the Champion Chase and Waterloo Boy the next day and then Desert Orchid in the Gold Cup.

'The hurdle track is tricky especially in the Champion or Triumph. It is important not to get caught on the inner at the top of the hill with the early leaders and pacesetters tiring and dropping back. Often it is not worth taking the shortest route because of this. You can't always get out when you need to. There's always a lot of scrimmaging for position and if you can see something going very well you might try to track it. On the Old Course which we race over for the first two days there are two hurdles down the hill and one in the home straight. Generally those in front at the last in the Champion Hurdle win.'

The thrill of riding a Festival winner does not diminish with age or regularity. Nor does the riding. It had been a great thrill as an amateur having his second ride at the meeting. His début had been on Bashful Lad in the Kim Muir earlier in the afternoon before he teamed up with Oyster Pond in 1984. He had gone a million miles an hour on the tearaway in the Grand Annual and still hadn't managed to lead the race. What a thrill it had been, beaten two and half lengths by Mossy Moore ridden by Jonjo O'Neill who earlier in the afternoon had won the Champion Hurdle on the famous mare Dawn Run. It had been a very big thrill the following year in 1985 when, in his first season as a professional, Von Trappe had won the Joe Coral Hurdle. Since then, the reception he had received on the Irish-trained Montelado in the 1992 Bumper had nearly surpassed the Gold Cup and Champion Hurdle. But each victory had, in its own right, been just as sweet and now, going out for the first race of the 1993 Festival to ride

Dreamer's Delight, the determination and resolve, the need to win, are greater than ever. In this game the more you win the more you want to win, it is an obsession.

Against Dreamer's Delight was Montelado, the ride of Irish Champion Charlie Swan. Richard had tried to get off Dreamer's Delight and on to Montelado again and again but the Duke, as was his right as his retaining trainer, refused each time he was asked. And fair dos, why retain someone if he's not going to ride for you. Dreamer's Delight is something of a character. At Doncaster the previous outing he had found nothing off the bridle up the run in, having looked assured of his fourth victory of the season. He had stopped up the hill at Sandown the time before in a thrilling finish when apparently clear of Sun Surfer who had rallied under a driving finish from Carl Llewellyn. Now in the Trafalgar House Supreme Novices' Hurdle over the Champion Hurdle course and distance he was to be fitted with blinkers to sharpen up this reoccurring trait in his style of racing.

Around the paddock, crowded by owners, trainers, travelling headlads and colourful jockeys, spectators line the rails three or four deep. In black and white stripes, emerald green and white striped sleeves Richard is given a leg up by the Duke, a deft, gentle movement of his right hand levering Richard's left leg and the jockey springs into the saddle. Such a simple easy-looking movement, a minimum of effort and movement from both, yet try legging up an overweight without any bounce in their legs and you'll rarely see a commotion like it. There is expectation in the air. Some devotees have waited 363 days for this.

The 35,000 take up favourite viewing positions. The lucky in private boxes, others in front of the television in the Turf Club, others in the Arkle bar, the unemployed jockeys in front of the box in the changing room, Robin Grey the commentator from his box above the stand, the majority from the grandstands and lawns that run down to the rails. A roar erupts as the starter lets them go.

Dreamer's Delight gives Richard a good ride, he's still going well down the hill. Out of the corner of his eye he can see Montelado running away, as certain a winner as you're ever likely to see at this stage in a race at Cheltenham. There is no time to get upset about that, Richard is still going well enough to be placed. He is towards the inner trying to get a run going to the second last between Neale

Doughty on Frickley and Peter Scudamore on Lemon's Mill. Scu jumps across him, suddenly there's a shortage of room, Dreamer's Delight momentarily drops his guard, loses concentration. He's too close to it, he's galloped into it, failed to get high enough. He's buzzed up that much more because of the occasion. An ordinary day, Sandown or Doncaster perhaps, and his reactions would have been quick enough but here, going flat out, faster than he's ever been before, the ground comes up quickly to him, quicker than he can think. Richard hits the ground with a bang and in a ball. He's rolling along the middle to inside of the course with the majority of a fifteen-runner field yet to gallop over him. It is like parking your car in the fast lane of the motorway. You're bound to get hit and whether or not you're a write off depends on your luck.

Up the hill the crowd roars itself to a crescendo; it is patently clear to Richard lying quietly on the ground with green-stained cap and breeches, the result of skidding through the turf, who has won. It is the Irish yelling for Montelado who is finishing twelve lengths clear of the field. Richard is annoyed on both counts, the winner and the fall but that's the way the cookie crumbles in this business. He's been kicked but saved from severe bruising by his body protector. At Plumpton he might have considered taking the day off but at Cheltenham never. He's like the gored bullfighter, the only way you'll take him willingly out of the ring is on a stretcher. He slowly rises to his feet. Brough Scott, Richard's prophet of doom lately, is standing by the hurdle. 'Who has won?' he asks of the journalist whose ear is pressed against a transistor radio. His reply only confirms what Richard already knows. The Festival has begun badly and he returns from his first ride in the back of a Landrover driven through the hospitality area. First blood to the Irish is reconfirmed with a resounding three cheers for Montelado in the winner's enclosure. For Richard it is an ignominious beginning.

Wonder Man, his ride in the next, the Waterford Castle Arkle Challenge Trophy, a two-mile novices' chase for future Champion Chasers, had been beaten by the red-hot favourite Sybillin last time out at Nottingham. Richard is resigned that it is going to be hard to reverse that form and find the required four and a half lengths to win here. There is however a chink of hope, already a rumour that Jimmy Fitzgerald's horses had not shown good results in their recent bloodtests is circulating. It offers a ray of hope but against Wonder Man is the fact that, though normally fluent, he is prone to the occasional bad blunder. In the race he jumps off in front and remains there. At the second last Richard is surprised nothing has come to him. The others ought to be making a challenge by now. Wonder Man pings that fence, his jockey looks round. Sybillin is clearly beaten so he kicks again round the last bend to make sure of it, trying to put the race beyond doubt. He cannot believe it when Travado, another of his rides, whom he had schooled upsides only the week before, looms upsides going to the last. Unbeknown to Richard when he had looked over his right shoulder at the second last, Travado and Jamie Osborne had just made a mistake and drifted onto the rails behind Wonder Man. Both horses meet the last long and land running but Travado soon begins to assert himself, just proving himself to be a length better on the day. Richard had finished where he had anticipated but beaten by the wrong horse. He had always been going to ride Wonder Man, it had been a long-term arrangement, and Nicky Henderson's horse had missed his prep race. Even when they had schooled he had gurgled so the signs had not been great. Despite finishing second, the fact that Travado has won heightens the frustration.

This year's Champion Hurdle is regarded as one of the most open for years. Had Mighty Mogul made it then he may have been a clear-cut favourite but some horses had dropped out and others had shown little worthwhile form. Flown, Richard's mount, was as much favourite because of doubts about the others as he was for his own ability. Richard's own gut feeling was that it was an open race, he could just as easily win as finish out of the placings, it is that tight. At the start, Flown kicks Kribensis. There was nothing either jockey could do, as it happens, although the jockey of the kicked usually gets a bollocking and there is no damage. But, increasingly over the season and now in the competitive atmosphere at Cheltenham, jockeys were lining up right on top of the tapes, no longer walking in. It is perhaps a trend which helps explain an incident at Aintree two and a half weeks later.

Everything goes well during the race. Richard has a good clear run despite the eighteen runners. Always prominent he manages to get a breather into Flown at the fourth last ready for the last threequarters of a mile. At the third last he moves upsides Jinxy Jack who has been

103

in the vanguard for much of the way. Downhill the runners stream flat out, Granville Again is going well, Royal Derbi's moved into a challenging position on the outside of Halkopous. Flown is swallowed up at the second last and though he runs on again up the hill as if he might be better over further, there are no excuses. Just not good enough as he is beaten nine and half lengths by the winner.

When Richard pulls up Scu is ecstatic. You might have guessed with hindsight that he knew Granville Again was his last big winner and his first major title for Martin Pipe. As he is led into the winner's enclosure at the foot of a cheering amphitheatre, Richard explains to Edward and Peter Winfield, Flown's owners, how the race had gone. Naturally they were all slightly disappointed. If the public think your horse is the best by putting their pockets where their mouths are then you tend to believe them.

With no ride in the Ritz Club and not allowed to ride in the Fulke Walwyn Kim Muir, a race restricted to amateurs, Richard has a further hour in which to reduce his weight to 10st to ride Manenda in the last, the American Express Gold Card Handicap Hurdle over three and a quarter miles. The weighing room is a haven for jockeys from outside but in the sauna now it is even quieter, left alone to reflect with his thoughts and frustrations, to hope for better luck tomorrow and to wind his left arm over the shoulder to ease the stiffness. He comes out briefly, towel draped around the waist, beads of sweat on his pale body, to watch Luke Harvey beaten a shorthead on Country Member by Givus a Buck in the Ritz Club. Then it is back in for another fifteen minutes. The sauna is good for the bruises picked up on Dreamer's Delight, the heat increasing the muscle blood flow which assists the deportation of acid waste products. Its detrimental effect is to drain strength as the reduction in fluid within muscles means that there is a more rapid build up of lactic acid and therefore a greater feeling of fatigue. Changed into his light gear, see-through breeches, light tights, light boots, he watches Tom Jenks provide the Duke with his first winner of the meeting with Strong Beau. He is passed out at scale weighing a pound overweight.

Manenda, a six-year-old mare owned by Colin Smith and trained by the Duke, is hard work. Richard pushes her for a long way. She is outpaced from the second last. Charlie Swan is behind him going to that flight but gets a great run up the inside on Fissure Seal on whom Richard had won at Christmas. He had hugged the rail all the way and at one stage had nearly been forced out into the path of the oncoming open ditch. Manenda finishes fifth. She's run a good race behind Fissure Seal.

Back in the changing room, Richard is among the last to change. What's the point of rushing, it'll be bloody hours before the traffic clears. Charlie Swan wishes him good night on his way to a bar to celebrate his and Ireland's double. 'Well done Charlie,' smiles Richard, genuinely pleased for his friend. Pale, tired, sore, frustrated that three horses he might have ridden had things been slightly different have won, he looks like he's been mugged down Heart Break Avenue. The drive home is quiet, Carol is shattered running up and down to the last obstacle all day with a heavy camera. Ciaran O'Toole is with them but keeps a low profile in the back. Normally talkative he can sense the disappointment. 'I've had worse days than that,' reflects Richard. He cites Dai Tegg as an example, having missed the ride on Flakey Dove and still seriously ill in hospital, he is a benchmark for someone far worse off than himself. In the end the three of them decide not to go out for supper. Instead they prefer to watch *Question of Sport* and *Alas Smith And Jones* on television. With 10st 3lb the following day and 10st on Thursday Richard cannot afford to indulge in too much supper. For Richard Dunwoody, day one of the 1993 Cheltenham Festival concludes when he falls asleep in front of the television.

Yesterday was an easy day by comparison. Today, Wednesday, Richard has six rides and a lightish weight. Over a slice of toast and coffee he thinks the day through to himself. 'Hebridean in the first will struggle to beat Scu's mount Lord Relic and Trainglot is a danger. Atone might be the best of the Irish.

'Barton Bank in the Sun Alliance may find the fences his biggest problem, Young Hustler – he might have had too much racing. Dakyn's Boy could run well but I should have the beating of him. Capability Brown – Adrian Maguire rides him as Scu's got on Young Hustler – has good form but is not one I will want to track.

'In the Coral Hurdle I ride Bishop's Island who would have an each-way chance. Olympian and Andrew's First look to be the two to beat. Bishop's Island ran all right at Warwick but hasn't been that fluent over hurdles.

'The Queen Mother Champion Chase should be very quick on this ground. Boro Smackeroo will make the running and jumps left handed, Fragrant Dawn will be handy as will Moment of Truth, Young Snugfit and Wingspan. Five horses that like to dictate from the front, a very quick race, I'll aim to jump out handy and sit in, get a position on Waterloo Boy.

'Travelling Wrong, the Duke's runner in the National Hunt Chase, should have every chance with John Durkan on, and Claxton Greene under Marcus [Armytage] is the one to beat. Star Actor runs in it from Nicky's yard and though he's not the most comfortable to ride he has already finished third at Cheltenham this year under Charlie Vigors.

'The Midmay–Belstone Fox runs in this. He's really come to himself and loves the fast ground. Should get the trip but he's won twice over a flat two miles at Doncaster and Newbury, I hope he gets the two and half. The dangers here are Kentish Piper which Declan Murphy rides as Carl, his normal pilot, has to ride Plat Reay for the Captain. He's a reasonable outsider. Galevilla Express probably doesn't run. Smartie Express could run very well after the smashing ride he gave me at Wincanton though he is out of the handicap.

'In the last, I ride Diplomatic for Mick O'Toole after he won the tug of war with Homer Scott to ride Rhythm Section. Micko says he's in great form so I'm expecting the best. Otherwise Heist looks the best of Irish and likely to start favourite.'

The jockeys' changing room at Cheltenham is spacious and is partitioned into corners. An hour before the first, the majority of jockeys will be changing. Mark Perrett, leaner and taller than Richard, wanders around in his boxer shorts looking for Ashfold Copse's colours for the second race. The valets clear away the cards at which they have been gambling and like corners in a boxing ring tend to their own men, providing anything from spare breeches to saddles and elastic bands and safety pins. The Buckinghams have a corner and Steve Winter, a London boot maker, helps them out as well as taking measurements for new boots; Pat Taylor has his corner; Steve Charlton looks after the northern lads behind a wall to the left; Nigel Hook has his boys immediately on the left as you enter. The Irish, most of them wearing shamrocks as it is St Patrick's day, spread themselves about. Richard Dunwoody sits far right, hidden as you enter by a wall. To his right is Simon McNeill and to his left Hywel Davies, Scu and Eccles. By the entrance to the sauna and showers are a set of red trial scales enabling the valets to make sure their jockeys have the correct weights before going to officially weigh out. Beside it is a wooden crate of 1lb and ½lb lead weights, square and flat. Girths, colours, some famous and recognizable, body protectors, jumpers, breeches and mufflers hang from pegs which are placed under saddle racks heaped with every shape and size of saddle conceivable, the comfortable twelve pounder, the middle-sized five pounder down to the minute synthetically made postage stamp. Atop farmhouse-sized tables are bucket-sized tins of saddle grease and tins of polish. Underneath are the empty colour bags of a hundred trainers. The place is a kaleidoscope of colours.

Off to the right if you turn back on yourself is the tea room. On offer: tea and coffee, soft drinks, make-your-own-sandwiches of rare beef, ham and chicken, bowls of coleslaw and salads, Mars Bars, fruit, loaves of fresh-cut bread. A feast fit for a king in comparison to some tracks. The room next to that is the ambulance room. Two beds await their first casualties of the day, curtains ready to be swung round to offer patients privacy.

Jockeys sit joking and talking in twos and threes, others watch the SIS repeats of yesterday's races. 'You do check my leathers all the time, don't you?' asks Hywel Davies of Tom Buckingham. A giant get-well card awaits the signatures of those riding today. It will be sent on to Dai Tegg. Outside on the weighing-room steps, under yellow hanging baskets of pansies and primroses, girlfriends chat, trainers congregate with press and owners. Billy Balf, who forty-seven years previously had led in Prince Regent's Gold Cup, reminisces to anyone who cares to listen. Carl Llewellyn chats to trainer Chris Broad, Tim Forster to the handicapper Christopher Mordaunt. Mrs Monica Dickinson, whose son Michael trained the first five home in the 1983 Gold Cup, exchanges views with her son-in-law, Thomas Tate.

Richard's first stop has been the ambulance room where Mary Bromily has treated his bruises from the first day. From there on to a hospitality 'chat' with Jim (J.A.) McGrath, Hotspur of the *Daily Telegraph*, as the interviewer. In the first, the Sun Alliance Novices' Hurdle, Hebridean feels the increasingly fast ground but the race goes to Carl Llewellyn on Nigel Twiston-Davies' Gaelstrom who beats Ben de Haan on Cath Walwyn's Cardinal Red. Lord Relic, the favourite, also felt the ground finishing third. The Duke had had two runners in the race, the other being Now Your Talkin who, under Graham McCourt, had finished nearer last than first and had occupied the same position for most of the way.

The next race is the Sun Alliance Novices' Chase, three miles for novices who one day will make up into Gold Cup runners. The firm ground accounts for the small field of nine which is further reduced by the withdrawal of Dakyn's Boy. As Richard weighs out to ride Barton Bank the Duke has a cut at Graham. 'Hand your licence in,' he says and he's not joking. He believes Graham has not given his horse a satisfactory ride and he continues to have a cut at the jockey.

The Sun Alliance is always an incident-packed race often characterized by a large number of fallers if the field is big. Capability Brown sets off at a blistering pace, he hits the first, hits the twelfth and is upsides Young Hustler when he buries Adrian Maguire at the second-last ditch, thumping the compact Irishman into the ground. Barton Bank is strangely off colour through the first circuit. Maybe it is the fast pace, maybe something's amiss but he is usually free running. Richard knows all is not well. Passing the stands after a circuit he gives him a reminder just to check he is not sulking. He does not respond and jumps the fence in front of the stands in a laboured manner, heavy in his hands. He pulls him up and walks him back towards the last fence. The Duke is already there and though Richard is still unclear as to what is wrong the oncoming trainer can already see a faint trickle of blood from Barton Bank's nose. Meanwhile Young Hustler is making the best of his way home to give Scu his second winner of the meeting.

On returning to the weighing room the stewards wish to enquire into the poor running of Barton Bank. Though they are doing a job to satisfy those who may have backed him, the 7–4 favourite, the Duke is angry. 'Bloody obvious what's wrong with him,' he says gruffly. He had made one mistake at the first and the strain placed upon the horse there may have initiated the problem.

That is not the end of the race. Mark Perrett and Adrian Maguire are brought back to the ambulance room, both badly shaken. Mark is very upset. Yesterday he was second in the Champion Hurdle, despite four winners at previous Festivals, it ranked as his greatest moment there. Today, Ashfold Copse, a horse with a big future and trained by Guy Harwood for whom Mark has worked for fourteen years, is killed. Words cannot describe how low the battered jockey feels. Adrian is to take the rest of the day off in the hope of making it back for tomorrow.

In the Coral Cup, Bishop's Island runs indifferently. He had, thought Richard, a good chance of finishing in the first six but he trails in with the last six. Carl Llewellyn, only eighty minutes earlier on a high after bringing Gaelstrom home in front, lies on the landing side of the third last. Andrew's First was making steady progress through the field when Gallateen fell in front of him. With a large field and space at a premium Andrew's First tries to avoid the obstacle ahead but fails and goes down too, tripped by Gallateen. It is an awkward fall and a horse's leg catches Carl in the shoulder, the force spinning him round. Whether that or just the impact caused the collar bone to break we'll be uncertain but when Carl stands up one shoulder is dropped lower than the other, partly to ease the pain. An expert, another jockey, could tell from the stands what he had done. He hopes it is bruising but he knows otherwise and the question now is whether or not he will be fit to ride Party Politics in the Grand National.

Richard has little time to get his breath back between races. He weighs in, flings the saddle on the table, whips off Lord Vestey's royal blue colours and puts on Peter Deeley's white and maroon jacket. John Buckingham has the same saddle waiting but with a heavier weight cloth and, floppy silk cap dangling over his eyes, Richard sits on the trial scales while 'Buck' adds another 2lbs to the cloth. He weighs out. 'Number seven, sir,' he says. The clerk of the scales looks at his notes, checks the colours. 'Richard Dunwoody, Waterloo Boy, 12st so that's 12st 1lb,' he thinks loud enough for Richard to correct any mistakes. 'Thank you, Richard,' he adds and the formality is over and the saddle wrapped with girths, pads and weight cloth are handed to the waiting Duke. Richard grabs a half cup of tea from Sandy in the tea room adding his own sugar and a slice of a Mars Bar. He catches the end of the previous race on the replay, catches Carl's fall. He returns to his seat and is about to sit down, one moment to give the legs a rest, when the jockeys are called to get ready for the fourth race, the Queen Mother Champion Chase.

Richard has never won this race though he's had some wonderful rides, first on Very Promising and then on Waterloo Boy who is running in the race for the third time. In 1987, Very Promising had a titanic battle with Pearlyman. He had looked all over the winner but Very Promising had run back at him up the hill and just failed. He was never as good after that, almost as if Pearlyman had broken his heart. Memories.

He jokes with Simon McNeill who rides Katabatic. On paper it will be a two-horse race between the pair. Two miles on fast ground though, they are going to go one hell of a gallop. Waterloo Boy has run like a hero all season but doesn't like the fast ground. He does not give Richard his usual feel and does not jump as fluently as he is capable. Nevertheless he still has a chance at the top of the hill. Soon afterwards though, at the third last, he is beaten. He fades to finish sixth behind Deep Sensation who is given the coolest of rides under Declan Murphy, who kids his mount to beat Cyphrate threequarters of a length with Katabatic two lengths away in fourth.

After the Queen Mother Champion Chase Richard can afford to sit down for a while. The meeting is getting increasingly frustrating. Waterloo Boy had bled very slightly. But against the disappointments and let downs he appreciates that he shouldn't moan. 'Look at Dai Tegg, look at Carl,' he repeats. 'At least I'm in one bit.' Carl is now changed and strapped up, his empty coat sleeve dangles limply to his side. He is not sure the full extent of the break but he is very philosophical. 'I've had a winner, I can't complain, it's racing isn't it,' he says with the faint trace of a Welsh accent. The National Hunt Chase is for amateurs and it is a stirring finish after four miles with myself on the long-time leader Claxton Greene just failing to get back up and collar Ushers Island. Richard watches it already changed into Belstone Fox's blue colours.

Steve Smith-Eccles has been called up to ride Emsee-H in the Mildmay of Flete, as Adrian Maguire is injured. He has been speaking in hospitality most of the day and is in high spirits. In the race 'Eccy' is an early casualty. He leads to the first, Emsee-H jumps very badly right at it leaving Eccy hanging out the left-hand side-door. The horse bounces off the one immediately to his right and like something out of a comedy, Eccy who is recovering suddenly finds himself shot out over the right-hand side having over-compensated. Belstone Fox, who has given Richard a fine view of Emsee-H's departure, is left in front but is hampered by the loose horse around the long bend into the straight. At the fence in front of the stand Belstone Fox makes a complete horlicks, hitting the fence hard and low and landing unbalanced (see photos). Both horse and rider do their bit for self-preservation, Belstone Fox finding a leg and Richard sitting very quietly to prevent any further imbalance of weight. However mistakes such as this do not enhance a horse's chances and another error at the ditch – you could hardly blame him for a loss of confidence – puts him out of contention to finish last.

In the last Richard thinks he has a good chance on Diplomatic. His orders are not to rush it. Even if he finds the horse not travelling well he will run on, he has been told. This bumper is a popular race with the senior professionals, it is the only one they are allowed to ride in. They can pull their leathers up a few holes and play flat jockeys, it is the last race and there are no fences, a race for a bit of sport. However, those on horses with a chance have to take it seriously and up the hill on the far side Richard finds Diplomatic hanging in behind the others. He niggles at his mount and finds little response until turning the home bend by which time it is too late. Rhythm Section, under Paul Carberry, the horse he could have ridden, has already gone for home and beats the fast finishing Heist by half a length to lead home an Irish one-two-three. Richard is furious for choosing the wrong one. Charlie Swan, so the Irish punters thought, had left it too late on Heist, hero yesterday, villain today. Eccy had wished he had stayed in the hospitality tent after this race, his mount having given him a nightmare ride. Strong early on, it was climbing all over the horses in front of it and most of the jockeys agreed the race, with so many green horses in it, had not been as much fun as they had anticipated, the danger element just as great had there been fences to be jumped.

You spoke to Richard that night if you dared. The facial expression did not invite questions. Sure, he was only cross with himself. It was after all his choice but now, after two days of the Cheltenham Festival, two winners had got away, maybe four under different circumstances, and that, to Richard Dunwoody, is unacceptable.

Thursday, the third and final day at the Cheltenham Festival, attracts a crowd of 50,000. The phone rings early at home. Robert Kingston is on the line. Another Coral, his Gold Cup mount, has been found to be lame. 'You'd better ring Pipey,' says Richard. 'OK,' replies Robert.

Martin Pipe had, three weeks earlier, asked if he might be available for one of his three runners in the Gold Cup. Richard was contracted to ride Another Coral and thought he had a reasonable chance anyway if he saw the trip out. A specialist two-and-a-half miler, he would have the advantage of a turn of foot over most of the stayers in the race providing they did not sap too much energy from him before they turned for home. However in his last gallop he had strained a tendon and it had not shown up until the morning of the race. He could not be risked. Suddenly Richard was without a ride in racing's blue riband.

Robert sorted it out with Martin. He would ride Rushing Wild instead of Jonathon Lower, Scu's understudy in the yard. Richard regularly rode Shanagary, the owner's other horse, kept in training with Ron Hodges. It was to have been the biggest ride of Jonathon's career and, six hours before he was due to line up for a once in a lifetime shot at glory, he was broken the bad news that Richard had become available. For Jonathon it was like a relation had just died. This though is a dog-eat-dog business, no time for compassion although Richard would have to 'look after' Jonathon with a present afterwards.

There were other rides first and favourites to be ridden on the virtually virgin turf of the New Course first. In the twenty-five runner *Daily Express* Triumph Hurdle, Beauchamp Grace, bidding to become the first filly to win it, makes a bad mistake at the first. After that she hangs right, never travels and fades in the scrum to finish seventeenth. Up front Charlie Swan is adding to the Irish tally by bringing Shawiya home and it is her and not Beauchamp Grace who becomes the first filly to win the race. Baydon Star, another favourite, runs a good race in the Bonusprint Stayers Hurdle. Going to the last he looks all over the winner but under pressure there he makes a mistake, lands flat footed and is outstayed up the hill by Shuil Ar Aghaidh and that man Charlie Swan again. The first two races have gone to Ireland and the place is abuzz with Irishmen from all walks of life, from Waterford to Donegal, from Dundalk to Galway.

Richard is about to have his seventh ride in the Gold Cup. His first had been on the enigmatic Von Trappe, brilliant when he got his jumping together, but otherwise he usually ended up on the floor as he had done in Dawn Run's Gold Cup in 1986. 'He'd fallen at the fourth last. I remember walking down the hill and hearing this almighty roar from the crowd as Jonjo hit the front. I thought, that's it she's won, then the stands went almost quiet as Wayward Lad took it up between the last two. Then the roar returned, lifted the stands, I've never heard anything like it and you could tell the mare was getting back up. It was a historic day.'

Charter Party fell in his first Gold Cup the following season. It was The Thinker's year. 'It had started snowing during the Foxhunters and by the time we got to the start the snow was balling in their feet. As the forecast was for it to clear we returned to the weighing room soaking wet to wait for it to ease off. They used helicopters to help blow the snow off the fences, the take-offs and landings. Otherwise between fences we were galloping in snow. Charter Party, whose jumping took a while to come together, fell at the first ditch and I ran back to watch the race from the last.'

In 1988 Charter Party had won it beating Cavvies Clown six lengths. 'During the race he travelled really well and being on the bridle for most of the way helped his jumping which remained iffy until he retired. Cavvies Clown made a horrendous mistake at the second last which gave us the race on a plate. Charter Party was a much better Gold Cup winner than he was ever given credit for. He constantly suffered from navicular which makes horses lame. That day when I got on him in the paddock his lad, Dan Jones, said he hadn't taken a lame step all day and I knew then that he'd have a hell of a chance. It was a great training performance of the Duke to produce him sound on the one day that mattered most. Without his problems he'd have been a great horse and I'm sure a better jumper. Winning the Gold Cup was a great thrill and a very special occasion for the Duke.'

The following year it had rained hard throughout the Thursday and the course was heavily flooded by the last hurdle. David Elsworth and connections were seriously thinking of not running Desert Orchid in the appalling conditions. Richard again rode Charter Party who finished third. But up front one of the all time great stories of National Hunt was taking place. Desert Orchid had been passed by Yahoo at the last and as they splashed away from it up the long hill, both horses incredibly tired, Dessie began to fight back. He was already a folk-hero and this sealed it. The crowd went mad and a large number of hats cannot have been returned to their rightful owners' heads after that.

In 1990 Richard was now riding Desert Orchid following Simon Sherwood's retirement. 'I didn't think we could get beat,' he recalls. 'He went a circuit very well and I thought he'd only have to keep it up but he was headed seven out, carried wide into the straight, but at the second last we were still upsides Norton's Coin and Toby Tobias. I asked for one last effort and it just wasn't quite there. We were beaten half a length and four lengths. I had ridden Norton's Coin in the past and he was beaten in a handicap at Newbury before winning the Gold Cup at 100–1. I think everyone who ever rode him knew he had a great deal of ability on his day. In 1991 Desert Orchid was beaten a long way out in the race won by Garrison Savannah but he ran on very bravely to finish third beaten fifteen lengths. Though Dessie could go round the rail and didn't hang I think he had a marginal preference for right-handed tracks.'

In the changing room the jockeys are called out for the race. 'Jockeys out for the third, come on gentlemen.' The riders for the 1993 Tote Gold Cup finish polishing their goggles. Steve Smith-Eccles cracks his whip against his leg with cavalier determination, Peter Scudamore continues staring at the ground the rest of the world shut out, Hywel Davies makes a point of touching wood. Mark Dwyer, his body protector making him look barrel-chested, walks to the door while Richard Dunwoody takes one last look in the mirror, not with the vanity of a society hostess, just the habit of a professional perfectionist. Gold Cup or selling plate, in this business it is part of the job to look smart and tidy.

'You can tell it's the Gold Cup,' says John Buckingham who knows the jockeys better than most of their mothers, 'they're all so bloody quiet.' He knows this is not the time to crack a joke, not even to Steve Smith-Eccles.

Across the room Mark Pitman wishes Adam Kondrat, the French jockey, luck before joining Ben de Haan to walk out to meet Mrs Pitman. A pensive Jimmy Frost – he only needs this one to complete the set: Grand National, Champion Hurdle and Gold Cup – paces up and down, waiting.

Mark Perrett flexes his whip, inspects the flap. He's dripping with sweat from a hard ride on Pragada in the previous race, beads of it roll down his drawn cheeks. He's already had a week which would have given lesser men the emotional bends, second in the Champion on Tuesday, numbing fall that killed his horse on Wednesday, you wonder what might happen this time.

Adrian Maguire, who couldn't walk but only shuffled out of the weighing room the previous evening after Capability Brown had driven him backside first into the ground in the Sun Alliance chase, is now sound, warmed up after Major Bugler's Triumph Hurdle run and after threequarters of an hour of intensive physiotherapy with Mary Bromily in the medical room earlier that morning. To think that racecourse physios are an innovation.

There's a camaraderie about this band of sixteen men going to do battle. It's peculiar if you think about it, sixteen jockeys leaving the changing room with a team spirit that would do an international rugby squad proud and yet, out there, no quarter will be given. None of them is thinking he might be brought back on a stretcher, none will have worked out the winning jockey's percentage of the prize-money. Let's face it, they'd do this for free, just sixteen warriors with tunnel vision at the end of which is jump racing's blue riband.

They leave behind mixed emotions in the changing room. Compare their excitement with the unseen envy of those who long to be out there with them, other professionals and amateurs, bigger and heavier, waiting for the Christies Foxhunters. Some of them wishing, but for nature, that they too might have been light enough to make a living out of their hobbies.

And contrast it all with the bitter disappointment of those who might have been out there but for some misfortune. Anthony Tory, who used to ride for Kim Bailey, how would he feel if Docklands Express wins when six weeks ago he might reasonably have expected the ride? Jonathon Lower, how would he feel if Rushing Wild won? Six hours ago he was riding the horse now he's straightening his tie, about to go home. He's packed his bags and is ready to leave the moment the race is over. You think it would be marginally less agonizing for him to leave before it begins. James Railton, looking forward to his first ride in the race only to find out after the Triumph Hurdle that King's Fountain has arrived at the course lame.

Carl Llewellyn, his wing strapped across his chest, is smiling and joking. He has a glass of champagne. We shouldn't feel sorry for him and he's the last person to want that too. Last year he won the National when Andy Adams was injured. Now the boot is on the other foot and he'll have to sit it out, but he's had twenty-four hours to resign himself to it. 'Could have been worse,' he says.

For the race they gather round the changing room's two screens. Some sit on benches, others sit cross-legged on the floor, gripped initially in silence by the unfolding drama while a camera crew, filming a documentary called *Jockeys*, watches the watching. A cup of tea is placed on the table so it doesn't get knocked over in the excitement.

There are 'Oohs' when Run For Free clouts the downhill fence, audible 'Ows' when Cherrykino mistimes the ditch. 'Shit, that's H,' says someone before the commentator has picked up Hywel Davies's horrible fall. At the top of the hill the names of horses are picked out. 'Jodami,' says someone pointing to the screen. 'Rushing Wild is not stopping. Docklands wins nothing. That's done Garrison Savannah. Go on Mark.' The comments get louder, more vociferous. They urge Mark Dwyer on. No-one knows the facts but there are a lot of people hurting at the apparent injustice to Jonathon Lower in that changing room and even Richard's friends join in the crescendo urging Jodami home.

Rushing Wild had looked fantastic in the paddock. In the race he was proving it. He jumped off near enough the front, jumping very slightly right at a few fences as Richard had been warned. Sibton Abbey is about the only horse Richard really sees after Run For Free's mistake. At the top of the hill Richard has kicked for the final time, it's a long way from home but all Rushing Wild does is gallop. Turning in towards the second last he thinks he might even win. Then the big brown head of Jodami looms up alongside, he's running away. The crowd roar, jockeys cheer in the changing room, forty or so of them riding with Mark Dwyer to the last, riding his finish for him. Richard drives Rushing Wild at the last, lands running but so does Jodami. Head down he hopes to outbattle Jodami up the hill but it is wishful thinking, a vain hope. He pulls up and slaps a congratulatory pat on Mark Dwyer's shoulder. Both jockeys are delighted.

The jockeys return to the changing room. David Bridgwater grins, thrilled at finishing tenth. He's acquitted himself well, he's been blooded with the big time and he'll want to do it again. He's a good young jockey being given chances, he'll take those chances and mature for the experience. Jamie Osborne looks disappointed, few of his Cheltenhams will ever live up to the previous year when he rode five winners there.

Richard grins too, that ride has made an otherwise unsuccessful meeting for him. He has no excuses. Scu's philosophical. 'Did a Carvill's Hill at the first,' he laughs with Richard who talks him through Rushing Wild's race. 'Won't be far away next year,' says Richard. 'I can't wait that long,' says Scu. No-one notices the hint. Steve Smith-Eccles swears Sibton Abbey will win the race next year.

At the other end of the room Mark Dwyer returns to the northern corner, to cheers. Hywel Davies is brought back in the ambulance, concussed but still talking, only now more rubbish than before. Touching wood didn't work this time.

'Where are you tomorrow, Jamie?' asks Buck as he gives Jamie Osborne a hand off with Docklands Express' blue and yellow jacket. Outside Mark Dwyer and the connections of Jodami are being presented with the Gold Cup.

'Wolverhampton or Lingfield, I don't know.' He says it as if he doesn't care either. His next chance to win the Gold Cup is now 365 days away and tomorrow it will be back to reality.

Richard's day is not over yet. Viking Flagship is a non-runner in the Grand Annual and he swaps on to the Duke's other runner Shamana. She makes a mistake at the ditch, is outpaced down the hill but is only beaten two lengths by Space Fair. Tinryland makes a couple of errors in the Cathcart. He tracks The Illywhacker into the tenth fence. Mark Pitman growls at his mount which frightens Tinryland into taking off. Ironically The Illywhacker ignores the encouragement, fails to pick up and gives Percy no chance. Tinryland does not visibly break a blood vessel but the symptoms are evident to Richard and in his own time he pops him home. Perhaps he should have pulled him up. Up ahead another great roar goes up as the Irish record their sixth winner of the meeting with Second Schedual. Adrian Maguire's recovery seems complete – he has ridden both Space Fair and Second Schedual.

Richard has one race left in which to get on the score sheet, the Tote County Hurdle. He is 2lb overweight for Nicky Henderson's Thumbs Up. He wanted to be strong today because of the Gold Cup, therefore being a pound heavier was necessary. The field stream down the hill at a tremendous clip, already some of the die-hard spectators are leaving the course in a bid to beat the traffic, worse on Gold Cup day than any other. Spinning makes the running, is still in front down the hill. Duharra makes a terrible mistake at the second last and had he fallen Thumbs Up and Richard would have ended the meeting where it had begun, on the floor at the second last. Thumbs Up is running away, few horses have ever been going this well going to the last. Richard is still restraining him. He knows the horse is a character and that he may stop in front. He lands safely over the last and flings everything at the horse, reins, legs, arms, everything except the whip and their momentum carries them up the hill six lengths clear of the fast finishing High Baron.

The thrill of winning doesn't diminish. After these three days the sensation is heightened. The normally unemotional jockey can't hide his delight, punching the air and playing to the crowd who hang over the rails on the walk down past the stands to the winner's enclosure. His relief is tangible.

Thursday evening, the party's over. No-one else is around. There's half a bottle of Mark Dwyer's champagne, one of 12,000 bottles sold during the three days, on the valets' table. Richard, tired, exhausted, hungry, elated, finishes that off while he receives physiotherapy from Rabbit Slattery. Everyone else has gone. Michael Caulfield and Richard Phillips wander through the changing room. The jockey's pension adviser, who is with them, looks the worse for wear. He looks how Richard feels.

Outside old newspapers and discarded betting slips blow across the lawn in front of the grandstand. Catering staff load empties into a lorry, 18,000 bottles of wine consumed, 10,000 gallons of draught beer, 54,000 bottles of beer, 65,000 bottles of mineral water, 2,000 gallons of tea over three days. The fish-and-chip bar closes, he's sold a percentage of the 14,000 portions of fish and chips, not to mention a few of the 20,000 hamburgers and 35,000 sandwiches. Nightfall descends on Cleeve Hill, its normally quiet lanes illuminated by racegoers returning home. The old, the young and the middle aged tumble out of the Arkle bar, making more noise than perhaps they realize. In the tented village the merry-go-round revolves, its surefooted mechanical horses meeting every obstacle in perfect stride, to the tune of a barrel organ. The car park smells of petrol fumes as tired drivers rev to hold their position in the queue up the bank to the exit.

In the changing room Richard Dunwoody sits in his corner of the changing room, the last out of the shower, the last to change, drained.

CHAPTER EIGHT

WOLVERHAMPTON, THE DAY AFTER the Festival has finished, is flat, devoid of character. No matter that the sun is shining and the ground is fast, it is like a glass of lemonade which has been left standing all night. Wolverhampton after Cheltenham is the balloon after it has been burst, a joke without a punchline. It is an old story but there's more atmosphere on the moon. It never was the most inspiring racecourse that ever lived. Some good horses have run there but not in great races. The town itself is ugly and the backdrop to the course is a monument to the Industrial Revolution, a railway siding up upon a bank, a tall red brick viaduct, a memorial to the engineeers who built it. Few jockeys would mourn its passing save the fact that without the gaffs you wouldn't appreciate the Cheltenhams or Newburys quite as much.

In the square weighing room most jockeys feel the let-down. It's like eating at a Little Chef after dining at the Ritz, like playing cricket on the village green after Lords, it's like performing for the Stanford-in-the-Vale players in the village hall after playing lead for the Royal Shakespeare Company at Stratford. There's less pressure, more space on the stands, one man and his dog watching, but the jockeys would all prefer the power, the glory, the competition, the pressure of performing as they had done the day before, the chance of a more lasting fame, a better prize. Richard rides a double which at the end of the day will leave him 140–123 ahead of Scu but it doesn't really help to lift the spirits.

Saturday picks up. Racing is at Uttoxeter, a small track in Staffordshire. This particular day they are holding the Midlands National, a four and quarter mile handicap chase, two weeks before the real thing at Aintree, and it is the course's big day. Locals pack the stands shoulder to shoulder, the cramped conditions are a tribute to the course's management. Word has it that Stan Clarke is so meticulous that when he checks round the morning before a meeting he even inspects under the loo seats. Attention to detail has won him and his track a new-found popularity and that in turn generates a healthier, keener, bustling atmosphere. There's a small fun fair in the centre of the course, even young children would enjoy themselves at Uttoxeter.

On Channel Four's *Morning Line*, John McCririck, announcing that Richard is riding the day's 'steamer' Lake Mission for Simon Sherwood, points out how essential it is that the jockey rides at the correct weight 10st 1lb having seen that he did 10st 2lb on Thumbs Up two days before. 'I don't want to put pressure on,' he says in his flamboyant style knowing full well it will do just that. Lake Mission, is beaten twelve lengths by General Pershing into third, carrying no overweight.

In the next he has another ride for Simon Sherwood, the novice chaser Red Amber. His form figures include a couple of wins, a fall and an unseated. 'The fall should be an unseated,' Sherwood says to Richard. 'He looks after himself and is too clever by half to put himself on the floor.' Famous last words. At the last with a circuit still to race, Red Amber slithers along on his belly, eventually rolling on to his side. It is a soft-looking fall for Richard, lowered to the ground with precision, this is not a 40 mph pummelling, this is a gentleman's fall or so it seems.

However, as so often seems the case in this sport the softer falls cause the worse injuries. In reality it is Richard's pride, his inbuilt instinct for survival and ballet star's balance that gets him into trouble.

Instead of stepping off Red Amber, he stays with him on the deck, hoping he'll find a leg and get up again. Instead of being thrown clear Red Amber rolls and Richard ends up underneath him. Whether it was the reins rushing through his hands or Red Amber's foot he will never know, but besides the normal couple of bruises, his right wrist was immediately sore and a broken wrist can keep you off games for up to twelve weeks.

In the heat of battle when your blood is up adrenalin numbs the aches and pains. 'I feel fine,' Richard tells the doctor. He doesn't feel very fine but certainly not injured enough to prevent him riding Windy Ways in the Midlands National. His hand is sore, it just doesn't feel quite right and its movement is not quite what it should be. Windy Ways doesn't run well and finishes very tired, pulled up. It is nothing to do with the injury Richard is carrying.

The next race is a mares' novices' chase and Richard decides to give Barrica a miss. She pulls up so he has missed nothing spectacular but his hand is something of a worry. In the past jockeys have always avoided doctors. Attitudes are changing. It is now more of a partner-ship but not so long ago you'd bluff your way past them, they were seen as a barrier between you and your living. The need to put on a brave face no longer exists. He consults the doctor, they discuss it. He could send Richard for an X-ray but Richard suggests it is nothing Mary Bromily won't be able to put right on Sunday morning.

That night he and Carol dine at the Thai Orchid in Oxford with a few friends including Brendan Powell, still recovering from a broken leg. 'Looks bust to me,' he says. He's no doctor, Brendan, but when it comes to fractures he has a good collection, even by a jockey's standards. He passed the doctor after a fall at Aintree one day, just before a Grand National, and was about to drive himself home to Lambourn. He would, he assured the course doctor, see his local doctor when he got home if he was still sore. He'd had a terrible-looking fall and was sheet white. Externally there appeared nothing wrong with him and though he felt rough he thought he'd make it home all right. Changed, washed and ready to go he took a swig of Coca-Cola and with that collapsed in pain on the chang-ing room floor, dying. He had ruptured his stomach in the fall. Had he taken the drink in the car on the way home, the doctors said, he might not be with us now.

So jockeys have, to a large extent, mixed prudence and common sense and come up with a cocktail that has cured their allergy to doctors. No longer are they regarded with suspicion, now they are allies. You can discuss a sore or an ache with them without the worry of being stood down. Mary Bromily, however, believes the injury should be all right with more treatment, lasers, electric pulses, heat to reduce the swelling.

On Monday, Richard rides two seconds at Plumpton. Normally when he rides the reins are held between his thumb and index finger, fed along the palm of his hand, and out between the third and fourth fingers. Effectively he rides with three fingers. Now, to compensate for the pain, he rides on two fingers. It makes little difference, nothing that we'd notice, and the only difference it makes to Richard is that after a life-time of riding on three fingers it feels strange. For a day or two he will use his whip in his left hand until the pain has died down. Simple, a bit of improvisation.

The show moves on to Fontwell, a little left-handed track in Sussex. He is now acutely aware that the twice-a-day treatment to his hand is making little difference. Pennethorne Place is his ride in the first. She pulls very hard but looks like upsetting the odds-on favourite at the last. However up the run-in she begins to hang to the right. There's only one thing for it, to pull the stick through to the right hand and give her a crack, there's no alternative. She is beaten two and half lengths. Richard pulls up with no feeling in his right hand below his wrist, what feeling there is above the wrist is a shooting, searing pain. Whatever the injury was, it was certainly worse now.

The racecourse doctor suggests X-rays. Richard deliberates. An X-ray might reveal a fracture that will cost him the championship, it's a result he will not want to know. On the other hand the injury is going to affect his riding and that too might cost him the championship. By this time he is feeling faint. His Wolverhampton winner from Friday, Miss Marigold, is in the next. He stands down and elects to go to Chichester Hospital. Miss Marigold meanwhile tries to run out at the first and refuse at the second. She eventually jumps it so left handed that she unseats Eamon Murphy, her substitute jockey. A blessing in disguise.

A telephone call to the hospital has ensured no waiting. It is in fact the quickest he has ever been in and out of a hospital. The doctor there, Nick Ashford, produces the X-rays which reveal a diagonal fracture at the wrist end of the fourth metacarpal bone. It is bad news and good news. Bad news that there is a breakage but good news that it is the fourth metacarpal which should be splinted by the parallel bones either side. When shown the X-ray Richard presumed he was looking at a three- to four-week rest. Dr Michael Turner, the Jockey Club's medical officer, suggests a week might do. This would mean that Richard would not only be able to ride at Aintree but that he would be back the following Tuesday for a few rides before going there. A week was a blow but it would only mean missing four days racing in the south, he'd still lead the championship at the end of it and he'd get a much needed break.

The injury had proved a blessing in disguise in more ways than one. He had been due to school Won't Be Gone Long, his National mount, at Towcester racecourse the Sunday before Fontwell. However he had rung Nicky Henderson to cancel in order that he get some treatment on the hand. Consequently Martin Lynch, a friend and regular rider for Robert Waley-Cohen, the owner, had stepped into the breach. Won't Be Gone Long is usually the safest of rides and Martin is a jockey of huge experience. However at the last ditch as you come up the hill the horse suffered a rush of blood to the head, took a crashing fall, burying himself and his substitute jockey. The horse was all right but Martin, who had only just returned from a broken pelvis, was in some discomfort, was taken to hospital where he was detained with cracked vertebrae and concussion. He wouldn't ride again that season.

The Friday following the X-rays, eight days before the Grand National, Richard missed a treble at Newbury. Bloody annoying. But later in the afternoon he flew to Belfast with Willie Thorne the snooker player (and one-time big punter and owner) to appear on *Anderson on the Box*, a chat show presented by Gerry Anderson on which Father Breen, 'The Breener', a famous Irish priest who had run a tipping column in a paper before the Cheltenham Festival was also a guest. It is a National preview and they show Richard's fall on West Tip in 1985 when he had led the field over Becher's for the second time. 'What's it like to be trampled on?' they ask. 'At the time,' he replies reliving the moment, 'you're absolutely gutted at having blown probably the best chance you'd ever get of winning the race.'

He stayed at the Europa Hotel. He had stayed there once before when he had been riding at Down Royal. Scu had been with him in the taxi on the way from the airport. When they asked to be taken to the Europa the taxi driver had told them that its biggest claim to fame was that it was the most bombed hotel in Europe. Scu didn't even bother checking in after that and went to stay with some friends instead.

On Saturday Richard joins Richard Pitman as a guest commentator for the BBC. He is not, in his own words, over-forthcoming with his comments though he improves as he relaxes through the afternoon. The television man's dream is the guest who responds to questions immediately so there are no long, pregnant pauses, it is preferable to talk before you think. It's even more the case on the radio. That is not really Richard's style. But though it is an avenue he'd one day like to travel down Richard's mind is on the championship. In the first race alone there are three runners which he has ridden this season. Also before he had gone on television he had hopped on the scales to see how much heavier he was after a couple of days off. He was 10st 7lb stripped, an increase in four days of 7lb or 5 per cent of his body-weight. That too was playing on his mind during the afternoon, especially as he hadn't had supper the night before in Ireland.

This particular weekend is special for all jockeys. Sunday is the night of their annual awards where jockeys vote for whom they think are the best practitioners amongst their number. It was introduced in 1990 by Michael Caulfield of the Jockeys Association along similar lines to the Professional Footballers Association's annual dinner and awards. To be voted the best jockey by your colleagues is surely the most meaningful honour that can be bestowed upon a racing horseman, besides which the dinner is the only occasion in the year when all the jockeys, the most successful and the least successful on the flat and over jumps, get to meet. With no jump racing in the south the next day it is also a chance for southern jump jockeys to let their hair down slightly.

Many attempt to make a weekend of it. Richard and Carol are staying at the Plaza on the Park where Michael has organized a good deal for the jockeys. Saturday night is spent eating out in Chinatown with a few friends, Simon McNeill, Martin Bosley and partners, Robert Kington, David Bridgwater. It is a chance to relax.

Nowadays the dedication required of jockeys means they rarely get to see the city lights.

The Hilton is bustling when Richard and Carol arrive for the awards. It is one of the greatest collections of jockeys you'll ever find from Lester Piggott, Pat Eddery, Frankie Dettori down to apprentices on the flat, from Peter Scudamore and Richard Dunwoody downwards of the jumping boys.

The award for Jump Jockey of the Year goes to Richard Dunwoody, for the second time in three years. It gives Richard as big a thrill as any he's had this season or last. Though the awards are still gathering pace in the press this is the most prestigious. The first year it was a shock and though it is more expected this year it is still a great honour.

It is, however, totally eclipsed by the award for Jockeys Personality of the Year which goes to Lester Piggott for the third consecutive time. As he makes his way forward to pick up his 'Lester' there's a showing of his greatest moments to the music of Tina Turner's *Simply the Best*. It is a most moving, almost historical, moment. Only the greatest have been admired like Lester has, Ali, Pele, Best, you can count them on one hand.

The dinner in the Hilton winds up at 1 a.m. and the stragglers return to the Plaza where a large number of the jockeys are staying. It just so happens that the footballers have held their equivalent awards the same evening and they too have a deal with the Plaza and a similar number are gathered in the bar. There's plenty to talk about, the footballers tower over the jockeys but sportsmen like a drink together and this was no exception.

At one stage an Irish friend of Lorcan Wyer produces a guitar and begins playing Irish folk songs. Everyone joins in. The bar's doing good trade and everyone appears happy, everything is orderly and correct.

At about 3.30 a.m. the fire alarm rings. A number of jockeys who've already gone to bed appear in dressing-gowns. The bar staff show no apparent concern which lead those still drinking to believe it is a hoax. The bar staff accuse the jockeys of setting off the alarm, the jockeys accuse the barmen, their way of getting the bar to clear. No-one really knows who or where the alarm has been set off but a fire engine arrives to check it out. When they have disappeared back to the station the alarm goes for a second time. The fire engines return, dressing-gown clad jockeys wander downstairs again. Richard and a few friends continue drinking at the bar which the staff wish to close now. Only the die-hards among the footballers and jockeys remain finishing their drinks. A few footballers have their own cans by this stage and one or two jockeys moan to the bar staff about it closing. It is one of those nights Richard did not want to end. He and most of his colleagues are in bed most nights at 10 p.m. Once a year you feel the need to blow out, see the dawn without going to bed and this, after the awards, was one of those occasions. However, the bar staff would hear none of it but the hard core remained, Richard, Simon McNeill, Roger Marley, Mick Fitzgerald, Johnny Kavanagh, Adrian Maguire and a few others.

The police, about five of them, arrived at about 4.30 a.m., apparently for the third time that evening. Although Richard had not seen them they had come with the fire engines. They had heard reports of brawling and wished everyone to go quietly to bed.

'Would you like to lead the way,' they ask Roger Marley who is nicknamed 'Bob' by his weighing colleagues after the well-known West Indian reggae singer, Bob Marley. When he started in racing everyone assumed the R stood for Robert not Roger. It had, as nicknames do, stuck.

'No,' he said, 'I'm a resident of the hotel and can go to bed when I like.'

He is asked again. Once more his reply is negative. He is grabbed by the arms and marched out, spreadeagled against the police van, searched and bundled in.

'How can you do that?' said Richard in disbelief standing up for Roger and as you do after a few whiskies. A momentous night was in the process of being spoiled by Roger's arrest for what seemingly amounted to a non-offence. 'You can't arrest someone for not going to bed,' added Richard.

'Shut up and go to bed quietly,' said the policeman.

On his way to the lift Richard, in frustration, slapped a pillar – as you do after a few whiskies – in a feeble gesture of defiance. 'Perhaps I swore as well,' he admits. However, the police did not consider it that feeble and before he had reached the lift he found himself in handcuffs. He puts up no resistance but as he too is pulled out to the van to join Roger he is pushed over some glasses which break. Though he still maintains that timely shove was the policemen's doing, it does not amuse his captors who are coming to the end of a long night shift. At one stage the roof of the van looked very like the sole of a Doc Marten boot.

At Paddington Green Station – it's usually the first place they take captured terrorists – they are both interviewed.

'Name?'

'Marley.'

'First name?'

'Bob.'

'Sorry. First name?'

'Roger.'

'I thought you said Bob? Why didn't you say that first time?'

'No, I'm from Yorkshire, you must have misheard me.'

'I'm from Yorkshire too and I didn't understand you.'

By this time Richard is trying to contain himself and one of the policemen, showing he at least was human, had to turn away to prevent himself from splitting his sides before the two jockeys were led away to their cells with a cup of tea.

The next morning after four hours sleep the two were read their charges and told that if they accept a caution they'll be let off any further action.

Wishing to forget the experience, they both accept and take a taxi back to the Plaza. Roger had comprehensively missed first lot at Jenny Pitman's, that's for sure. After fetching Carol, who'd left Richard to go to bed ten minutes before the incident, but had been briefed about it soon afterwards, they rounded off an eventful night with a full English breakfast. Good for the spirit but not for the weight. Stories, already taking on epic proportions, circulated the restaurant. 'Woody arrested,' they whispered, what a story.

By Monday night journalists from the *Mirror*, tipped off about the incident, tried 'doorstepping' Hyperion House, to no avail. The neighbours rang complaining of people in their gardens and inquisitive phone calls. On Tuesday morning, the day of his comeback and five days before the Grand National, the papers were full of it. For them, at the start of Grand National week it was perfect timing. Midsummer and this wouldn't have been a story. Again reporters tried waiting at his front door from 7 a.m. Little did they know that Richard had already left to ride out for Richard Phillips in the village. The jockey that waved at them when a small string of horses trotted by, had they been switched on, was their man.

He had already notified the Duke before he had read about it in the papers and though he had appeared to take it well he had rung Michael Caulfield to blast him for being irresponsible for his jockeys. How he is meant to look after each of the 700 guests attending the dinner is beyond me. Michael hadn't even stayed in the same hotel.

The whole episode was beginning to leave a sour taste though. Some ill-advised flat jockeys were saying that the voting for the awards had been rigged though they are counted by a firm of chartered accountants. They were upset George Duffield had not won an award.

Monday had been spent sweating hard. With this furore, it was essential to do his minimum weight. He was well aware that being overweight would add fuel to any fire that the tabloids cared to mention. At the races the Captain greets him to take the saddle for Amari King. Just to reiterate he has a dry sense of humour.

'My God, if only I'd known I wouldn't have booked you. I thought you were in bed by ten every night with a glass of milk.' Amari King likes Sandown and, despite a pound overweight at 10st 1lb, beats Love Anew by threequarters of a length. Aware of the significance of the race, his first since his hand was diagnosed broken and the first since Paddington Green, Richard gives him a ride with which even he is pleased. 'Not bad for a steaming alcoholic,' says the Captain afterwards.

Richard's next ride was, somewhat appropriately, named Musthaveaswig. His owners had presented Richard with a badge upon which the horse's name had been inscribed but he resists the temptation to wear it. He is normally strong in race, which might have proved a tester for the hand as Richard was still riding with two fingers as opposed to three; however, he drops the bit. Sandown is not an easy track for him but he jumps well save for a blunder at the third last, the Pond fence. Nevertheless he still runs out the two-and-a-half length winner. Half an hour later Shamana hacks up to complete a treble for the jockey.

Hounded as he had been by the tabloids and with a number of evermore fanciful stories circulating regarding Sunday night, Richard felt it better to issue an apology through the Press Association for the adverse publicity he had brought on the Jockeys Awards and his fellow jockeys.

CHAPTER NINE

APRIL

THE JOURNEY TO LIVERPOOL, the Thursday morning two days before the Grand National, makes your stomach tingle with excitement and anticipation, the thought that there's a chance you may be driving towards the greatest day of your life. It is the same for owners, trainers and jockeys alike. The race is already commanding great media attention in the form of previews, interviews with likely candidates for success and sweepstakes, while previous winners or obscure participants are dug out of the ground to recall their most famous day and *Sportsnight* runs its preview picking out a couple of interesting horses and their connections. Even the nudes in the tabloids are draped in silks and caps. It will come to a crescendo on Saturday morning with each newspaper producing a pull out on the race. Though there are other races at the meeting they, like all other races in the calendar, pale against the Grand National.

THE GRAND NATIONAL

It is not difficult to put your finger on the attraction of the Grand National to a jockey, a would-be champion or amateur. Firstly, it has such a long colourful history. Since Richard was born look no further than today's changing room and the valet therein. In 1967 John Buckingham steered Foinavon, at the time struggling at the back, round the pile-up at the twenty-third fence to bring his mount home, almost alone. Never in racing history has a race looked more like a battlefield, a failed cavalry charge. Then, of course, there was Red Rum in the Seventies. Three times a winner and if you speak to Brian Fletcher who rode him to his first two victories in 1973 and 1974 he'll tell you it should have been four. Red Rum was a godsend to the race at a time when the future of the course was in serious doubt after the redoubtable Mrs Topham had sold it to Bill Davies, a property developer.

Every year the race produces a screenwriter's story but in 1981 it surpassed them all with Bob Champion's National-inspired recovery from cancer to ride Aldaniti to success in front of a crowd swept along on a tide of emotion. It sealed the race's fairytale billing and was made into a film for the big screen, *Champions*. In 1982 forty-eight-year-old farmer Dick Saunders guided hunterchaser Grittar to the most convincing success in recent years to prove age no barrier and add another incredible chapter. A year later Corbiere won the race and Jenny Pitman became the first female to train a National winner.

Rhyme 'N' Reason's success in 1988 was amazing in that he slid along on his belly at Becher's Brook on the first circuit. Brendan Powell sat tight, gave him time to recover, coaxed him back into the race and to get up in the closing stages. A week earlier he had had his car stolen and for the first time Citroën were providing a car for the winning jockey. Every year you can pick out some sort of story: Mr Frisk, formerly so wild that he had to be led at exercise from another horse, Seagram, who could have been bought by the sponsoring company also called Seagram, Party Politics, a giant who took one stride to everyone else's two. Even West Tip had a good story. As a youngster he had been hit by a lorry which had taken a huge chunk out of his backside and the unsightly scars of that accident, which in many cases would have finished a career, still remain with him. It is the sense of history that we yearn to be a part of, when you ride in the race you want the next chapter to be about you.

Secondly, the National is a jockey's one chance to make it, albeit just for a weekend, outside his own sport, and for that matter to achieve an immortality within his own ranks, in one fell swoop achieving a fame that may take a champion jockey a season. It brings other benefits, appearances on television, a *Question of Sport*, a celebrity status which allows you to return to your own real world after a while. Jump jockeys are rarely in such demand and hardly ever in the national spotlight as they are through National week. Anyone with a ride in the race, however much of an outsider, is newsworthy. It focuses attention on the sport outside the racing pages.

Thirdly, we all need a challenge and the course, despite its alterations, still represents just that. Jumping park fences is the run-of-the-mill, the bread and butter of a jump jockey's diet. Sure, they are capable of giving you thrills, spills, the danger, the adrenalin when jumped at speed but nothing compares to the fences at Aintree, bigger, more inviting, the softer colour of green, the drops that require a different style and leave you hanging in the air for eternity, like riding through a still photograph, the big ditches, the virgin turf, the stimulation. And, though many jockeys don't like the alteration to Becher's, this place will for ever remain Aintree to them. There is no comparison to this Aintree in April.

Fourthly, for Lambourn jockeys, because it is a two-and-a-half-hour journey, with perhaps the exception of Ayr or Perth for their three-day meetings, it is the only racemeeting that allows us to stay away during the season. There are a number of popular hotels in Liverpool like the Adelphi, which in the old days the winners always went back to for a party after the race, the Prince of Wales in Southport, the Grosvenor in Chester. Hotels fluctuate in popularity like public houses. The Post House at Haydock remains a popular venue out of Liverpool itself and has been lucky for a number of jockeys recently including Richard. However, this time he had booked into the Thistle Hotel across the road, slightly less crowded and with the required sauna. It also has a steam room for variation and a pool.

Though the meeting is about one race, it has become more of a festival in its own right. It's a festival of secondary importance to Cheltenham but with increased sponsorship its races are valuable and often attract Cheltenham winners and winning at both meetings is still considered a great feat, the tracks being so different. The only similarity between the two is that they are left handed. Otherwise compared to undulating Prestbury, Liverpool is pancake flat and very sharp. Were it not for the prize-money and for the National course, the Mildmay course would not be popular as a riding venue among jockeys.

The National course, though, is what it is all about, Everest compared to Ben Nevis, Earl's Court compared to Sparsholt village hall, Wimbledon compared to Uffington Tennis Club. You start with your backs to the stands, a maximum field of forty, and charge down towards the first of thirty fences with four and a half miles ahead of you. In distance alone it is unique, being the longest chase. You cross the first landmark, the Melling Road, after about a furlong. The road has been covered over and its black grit kicks up in your face from the front runners as your horse struggles to get to grips with the sudden and brief change from turf. Some even attempt to jump it. You're trying to sort yourself out going to the first, getting a position, in search of daylight, trying to take in those colours which are indelibly inscribed on your mind of those horses you don't want to track. Now that the course has been altered the relative significance of the first fence as a problem has grown. Horses are invariably travelling too fast in search of a good position, a clear run at it. In fact it is probably no exaggeration to say you're travelling two mile pace at this stage, not the steady married man's gallop you'd expect of four and a half miles. With no gears you'll just have to hope and pray. The year before Richard won on West Tip he had picked out one horse to keep away from, Solihul Sport. At the Melling Road who should come past him, running away and out of control but Solihul Sport who jumped across West Tip and fell, but luckily away from him. Richard prefers the middle and it seems that there is more room here than there is on the inside, a popular and crowded route especially now that the drop has been levelled on the landing side of Becher's.

Over the first, four foot six inches, your mount seems suspended in mid-air in comparison to a park fence. You're both taken aback by the drop on landing, the need to slip your reins a few inches more than usual as the horse's nose comes perilously close to the ground. At the second, an inch higher, you hope he's beginning to adapt, get a hang of it. His first major surprise will be at the third, a five foot high fence the other side of a six-foot ditch. Most horses are very clever and learn rapidly. They'll recognize that this is bigger than they've ever jumped before and that they need to get closer to the fence before taking off in order that they reach the other side. Unlike The Chair there is a drop on the landing side. The fourth and fifth should not present a major problem after the first three. A jockey hopes by now that he and his horse are settled into a rhythm, his mount getting within a foot or six inches of the foot of the fence brushing through the top inches of spruce, he himself sitting back, slipping his reins, gathering them in one motion, one stride on landing, moving onward to the next.

Becher's Brook is the sixth. Some people used to tell me that they were so carried away they never noticed Becher's and upon landing over it thought they were in fact about to approach it. You know when Becher's is coming, that's all I can say. There's a long thorn hedge down the left-hand side of the approach, there a footpath to be crossed and a red flag flutters in the breeze above steeplechasing's most famous landmark. It is unmistakable even in the heat of battle. To your mount it must almost look like you're going to jump into the crowd on the landing side. Indeed were you to continue straight you would end up tangled up in the scaffolding of a BBC camera placement as the course bears left handed to the seventh. As a general rule Becher's is still steeper down the inside than it is on the outside. Another reason for not going tight to the inner is that horses generally drift to the left here to correct themselves. Hard against the rails you cut out this option and those that meet it wrong have no chance for they cannot drift left as Peter Scudamore found out on Strands of Gold once. The option of drifting right is out because the fence is angled across the course right to left. The idea of 'drifting' is to give the horse more space. Going right would mean you meeting the fence sooner.

You'll notice the long drop on landing. Even horses who jump it well will peck, their heads coming within inches of the ground. Becher's on the second circuit often catches out the leader, possibly because of the noise of the crowd (it rarely happens in the John Hughes when there is no crowd), and possibly after jumping twenty-one fences the concentration may be beginning to wane.

The next comes up upon you quickly, Foinavon's fence. At four
foot six inches it is the smallest fence and often the best jumpers
make a mistake here, perhaps because they are expecting Becher's
again, perhaps because it is smaller and they or their jockeys relax
too much, maybe because it is on an angle. But in 1967 this is where a
loose horse brought the field to a halt and reduced the fence to virtual
dust. It's then on to the Canal Turn. Unlike Foinavon's fence, you
meet it straight then turn 90 degrees to the left on landing. Again
you can get murdered on the inner here by horses swinging out and
then cutting the angle to save ground. Better to be the murderer in
this case though. Equally on the outside you can get pushed wide and
lose valuable lengths. One problem here, rarely pointed out though it
occurs nearly every year, is slipping tack. A horse that turns sharply,
maybe turned by another runner on its outside or following those in
front, may catch his jockey unawares and with all his weight suddenly
thrown to the right, he often finds his tack following his weight. West
Tip's saddle rocked momentarily here in 1986.

On the first circuit the Chair still awaits, five foot two inches
preceded by a six-foot ditch. It is also the narrowest fence on the
course and though the general assumption is that the field has had a
circuit to sort itself out after two miles, in reality they are probably
bunching up again after hunting round as jockeys seek a suitable
position to set off on the next circuit. The biggest difference between
the Chair and the other fences on the course is that the ground is built
up on the landing side and those horses looking for another drop can
be surprised by the ground coming up to meet them. In recent years
it has not proved a great hazard in the National and it usually claims
more casualties in the John Hughes where it is the third fence.

You always find a few glory merchants beginning to get carried
away at the start of the second circuit. They start racing too early,
want a slice of the glory, want to lead the field down towards Becher's,
wanting a piece of the action. Better though to bide your time down to
Becher's, then start squeezing them up before joining the race proper
and the front line after the Canal Turn.

Now heading for home some tired horses will start to pick up,
find a second wind with the psychological knowledge that home
can't be too far away now, the end in sight. Valentine's, a Becher's
clone but not jumped at such an awkward angle and without such a

drop, is next. Another plain fence at five foot follows, the tenth and twenty-sixth. On to what, on the second circuit, is the fourth last and final ditch, five foot with a six-foot gaping open ditch, often the last major obstacle between potential winner and winning post. Once over the third last and the Melling Road, the grandstands hove into view, still threequarters of a mile away but you are now back on the racecourse and have just two plain fences between yourself and that impossibly long run in. I say 'impossibly long' and it is on a horse that is coming to the end of its tether – ask Richard Pitman who rode Crisp or John Oaksey who rode Carrickbeg if it didn't seem like a thousand miles. And yet ride up there with plenty of horse underneath you and it's like a hundred-yard dash.

Richard had ridden in the Grand National eight times before 1993, every year since 1985 when he had had his first ride there on West Tip. Aintree brings out the best in some horses and West Tip was a prime example. A very good staying chaser in his own right he was not quite Gold Cup winning class (he was fourth in 1987) but, even in the later stages of his career when winning hunterchases at level weights around park courses was a struggle, he could go to Aintree and beat most of the best. In the Eighties he was without doubt the best Aintree specialist. In 1985 Richard cursed himself when West Tip fell whilst leading the field and looking like a winner at Becher's Brook on the second circuit. It is amazing how often this happens but West Tip went down with his ears still pricked even as he landed, as if distracted. 'I was absolutely gutted,' says Richard. 'West Tip was travelling so well, I really thought he was going well enough to win and I thought I'd blown my best opportunity of ever winning the race. Chances like that don't just happen as a matter of course. Look at poor old Jonjo O'Neill, a great jockey, who never completed the course. I lay there as if my world had fallen apart. I blamed myself. Now I always look for a lead over Becher's second time. The leader at that stage falls too often for it to be coincidence. But it was the only mistake West Tip ever made in five Nationals with me. He ran his sixth National with Peter Hobbs who again had a superb ride. I don't think he made one then either. He was just a natural round there, he'd pick out fallers before you did and edge away from them in mid-air. He was undoubtedly the best since Red Rum. You could leave it all to him. The plan in 1986 was not to hit the front until the elbow halfway up the run in. I was always travelling well and Chris Grant on Young Driver gave us a good lead. At twenty-two, I was probably too young to really appreciate and savour what was my greatest moment. I had dreamed about it, in Ireland as a child I'd even stayed away from the local point-to-points on National day so I could see all the build up on television.

'In '87 and '88 West Tip was fourth and I got a huge thrill when he was second again, to Little Polveir, in 1989. He had been hunting that season which had regalvanized him. He was beaten seven lengths and, though finishing second can be heartbreaking on occasions, he ran as well as he had ever done and we had no excuses.'

In 1990 Bigsun had looked a promising ride for Richard. He was a fast-ground specialist, a good jumper and with Richard and his previous record in the race was made second favourite to win. Back in February Richard had been asked to ride Mr Frisk by Kim Bailey. There appeared to be little between the two horses and Richard's contractual commitments to The Duke prevented his accepting. This proved a godsend to myself, the next choice of rider for Mr Frisk, and the ultimate beneficiary of Richard's unavailability. However the firm ground proved too fast and though Bigsun ran valiantly and put up a good performance, he was outpaced for much of the way, to finish sixth behind Mr Frisk and myself who shattered the course record by fourteen seconds on the firmest going Aintree had seen since the War. Surely Bigsun's turn would come the following year. He was just off the bridle in about seventh when, at Becher's second time he all but fell, slipping on his stomach. It was a feat of great skill and balance that he and Richard picked themselves up but the strain of recovery, trotting away from the fence, told on Bigsun and, his chance gone, Richard pulled him up at the Canal Turn. After that he never really regained his form.

In 1992 Richard was united with Brown Windsor for Nicky Henderson. He had been fourth to Mr Frisk but had injured a tendon in the process. Now though second favourite, largely on the strength of his first run in the race, he got no further than the dreaded Becher's first time. He had drifted left handed but the large Forest Ranger and Dai Tegg had kept straight in their approach. In a mid-air clash there was only ever going to be one loser, the smaller Brown Windsor.

With much of the course now drained, fast ground is going to be an increasingly common occurrence at Aintree. Richard drove up to Aintree with Carol, excited at the prospect of her first Grand National meeting as a photographer, and Aidan Murphy to whom a few summers earlier Richard had been best man. His wife Annabel King, with a small string of horses to look after, was going to make the journey up and join them at the Thistle Hotel, Haydock on Friday evening. Richard was not much worried by the ground which Won't Be Gone Long had proved in 1990 that he could handle. The fast ground, though, without which my success in 1990 would not have been possible, was going to be a disadvantage this year for Travel Over, a large old chaser whom I had been asked to ride by Richard Lee. The changing room at Aintree has changed little, I doubt, in the last fifty or hundred years. Dark wooden panelled walls, wooden bench seats that open up to provide locker spaces, greet you. It smells of history. Here changed the great National winners of the past, Fulke Walwyn, Bobby Petre, the first to win the race after the War, Fred Winter, Bryan Marshall, Arthur Thompson. They'd still recognize it, the uniqueness of it all. Here men who had left the room mere jockeys half an hour earlier had returned to a hero's reception, their lives changed in some way for ever. Winning the Grand National is something that always lives with you and when a winner dies the first thing they'll say in the obituary is that, regardless of his other feats, he won the National. Brian Fletcher had returned here, three times triumphant, Bob Champion had returned here to a room of grown men in tears, so moved had they been, here had Richard Dunwoody returned in 1986 as if floating in a dream.

If you have ever been lucky enough to win the race something touches you when you arrive at Aintree, past Speke Airport, past the factories of Liverpool's industrial suburbs, past signs to Fazackerley, past Vernon Pools, past colourful newspaper adverts hung from every lamp post within half a mile of the course, turn left into Melling Road and left again into the narrow path that brings you to the owners' and trainers' car park. If you've won the race this is your spiritual home and you share in its secrets. You somehow feel invincible there, you walk taller than everyone else with a bounce in your step, wink at the statue of Red Rum, look at the winner's enclosure and wish to be back there on Saturday, to savour the moments that passed so quickly last time.

Winter Squall runs all right in the opener, finishing fifth to Roll A Dollar. The track proves a little sharp for him. Belstone Fox makes another monumental error in the next and Richard decides to pull him up when he is out of contention. He has to be content watching the day's two big races, the Martell Cup and the John Hughes Memorial, on television in the changing room. Competition for rides in the latter is intense, as much so as it is for the National. Everyone wants a cut at these fences and for many a good ride round in this race will be the season's highlight. Richard had been offered Winabuck but he has not grown older without growing wiser. He declines the ride and though Winabuck does not fall the end result is the same when he is nearly brought down at the Chair and his jockey is knocked out of the sidedoor. Instead the race is won by the talented young Adrian Maguire who beats Chris Grant a neck in a spirited finish to deprive 'Granty' once more of Aintree glory, three times second in the National and now three times second in the John Hughes.

Kadi remembers the hustle and bustle of Cheltenham and the Triumph Hurdle. He beats only one home in the four-year-old hurdle and yet is only six lengths behind the winner. Pashto rounds off Richard's day with a third behind Andrew's First and Carl Llewellyn, who only two weeks and a day earlier had broken his collarbone, in the three-mile hurdle. Not the most satisfactory day but then with the National less than forty-eight hours away staying in one piece is essential. Last year the fences on the Mildmay course had been made too stiff which resulted in about four eleventh-hour substitutions for the National, including finding a jockey for the favourite Cool Ground.

Friday began with some confident riding from Graham Bradley on Black Humour in the first and Declan Murphy again kidding Deep Sensation home in front in the Mumm Melling Chase, waiting and waiting when most of us would have gone for gold. Waterloo Boy, perhaps at the end of a long season, burst a blood vessel after a circuit. Richard knows something is wrong but it is not until colleague James Railton points it out to him at the end of the back straight. The problem is confirmed when Richard sees his breeches are speckled with blood. He pulls him up as soon as possible.

At the start of the three-mile handicap hurdle a crowd of Liverpud-lians with deep Scouse accents barrack Scu. He had been beaten on Young Hustler, over the top after a long season, in the big novices' chase. 'You bast'd robber, Scudamore,' they shout, much to the mirth of the other jockeys who know full well they'd be on the receiving end of these fickle punters' bad language if they too had been riding a beaten hot favourite. 'Oi Scu, you robbed me. Givus our money back.'

After a circuit the race comes to an abrupt, tragic end for Richard's mount Now Your Talkin. On level ground his leg shatters. With a mile and a half to go he had not been under a huge amount of stress and the injury occurred away from a hurdle but, as sod's law decrees, in front of the stands. Horses injured in the heat of battle are usually incredibly calm after the initial shock. It is as if they don't feel pain after a short panic, just an irritation no worse than a bee sting. They remain calm, ears twitching until despatched by the vet's humane killer behind a green screen.

Friday evenings are traditionally spent at a local restaurant, the Travellers Rest. For some reason Carol, who does the organizing, always books the Huntsman's Lodge about fifteen miles in the op-posite direction because we forget the name of the Travellers. But in the past it has been lucky for us. We ate there in 1988 with Brendan Powell, in 1990 and again in 1992 with Carl who won the following day. One year Richard's car was broken into in the car park there and the thieves, in order to get round the anti-theft locking device, had just removed the steering wheel when they were disturbed. They were not, however, sporting enough to leave the wheel as they legged it and it was the following week before a new steering wheel could be found. There's an old girl behind the bar there who greets us every year like long-lost children and she'd be upset if we didn't go. It is not a late night with most of the jockeys doing light the next day.

The following morning Richard is up at 7.30 a.m. for a sweat. Some jockeys will have been at the course riding out their mounts but not with 10st to do. However, the need to be strong in this race outweighs considerations of minimum weight and he'll aim for 10st 1lb. He reads a selection of newspapers, each trying to outdo the other with their colour National supplements, as he alternates between the dry heat of the sauna and the wet of the steam room, occasionally taking a dip to cool off and refresh. There is no sauna at the races. He takes coffee and a slice of toast for breakfast.

He leaves the hotel at 10.30 a.m. and is at the course within half an hour. Viking Flagship is to be withdrawn from the second because it is too firm and Hebridean from the last for similar reasons, so he will have just two rides, Flown in the Martell Aintree Hurdle, a re-run of the Champion Hurdle, and Won't Be Gone Long in the big one. It is overcast when he gets to the track, rain is forecast.

He dodges from one interview to another, from John Inverdale on BBC Radio 5 to a local Liverpool station. Richard Pitman wants a word for SIS and a Japanese film crew give him a watch in gratitude. When word of the latter spreads there is a queue of jockeys wanting to be interviewed by the Japanese. He walks the course, it is part of the ritual. There's no need for him to familiarize himself with it, he could probably tell the yardage between the first and second fences, he rarely does it anywhere else nowadays – perhaps if there is time or advantage to be gained out of finding the best ground – but it helps pass the time of day, and he'll bump into a few friends on the way round. Carol jogs to keep up with her impatient, revved-up husband. He's in a hurry, waiting for no-one and in his own mind already out there guiding Won't Be Gone Long down towards Becher's, angling the Canal Turn, visualizing what's ahead.

Back in the changing room he reports for treatment to his hand. He had been due to ride Macarthur in the last the previous evening but after falling from the injured Now Your Talkin last night he had felt a twinge in his hand and had asked to be stood down. There was no doubt in his own mind about being able to ride but the BBC wanted an opening shot for *Grandstand* of him posing with a thumbs up signal and grin. He obliges.

Naturally with forty runners in the National the changing room is crowded. There is already a buzz of excitement in there, those jockeys with a real chance, others with a distant hope, some knowing it will take a repeat of Foinavon's year if they are to win and yet that possibility still remains. Anything can happen in this race. Traditionally each jockey gets the other thirty-nine to sign their racecard as a memento. It can take a long time and cards are handed in for charities so by lunchtime most will have signed a hundred racecards and sought out his thirty-nine colleagues. Just So is a non-runner which means one less to find. The television is on and the BBC show previews reviews of previous Nationals; it makes fascinating watching until they start showing a few spills or ground shots of fallers at the first.

Most of the jockeys are in there. Outside in the weighing room telegrams are posted on the wall for collection. There's one for Charlie Swan. Trainers come in and out, check the declarations, pick up racecards. Graham Welcome puts out the neatly pressed number cloths on a table awaiting collection from jockeys when they weigh out.

Josef Brecka, the Czech rider whose town has sponsored his ambition to ride in the National after winning the Velka Pardubice, speaks pigeon English to the valets. Jonathon Lower, jocked off in the Gold Cup, now has the ride on Chatam, undoubtedly one of the best horses in the field but not guaranteed to jump round now he has his chance to show the world. Scu could have ridden him but has opted for Nigel Twiston-Davies' Captain Dibble, the race favourite. Carl Llewellyn, as relaxed as ever, no pressure on him, he's won it before and he didn't really feel the pressure then. Ben de Haan won it in 1983, a decade earlier and now on Gold Cup third Royal Athlete chats away to Mark Pitman who rides Garrison Savannah, second in 1991. Robbie Supple, another cool customer, with a great chance on Zeta's Lad unbeaten in five outings this season, gossips to fellow Irishman Conor O'Dwyer who rides Laura's Beau. Neale Doughty has the finest record in the race and has wasted away to do 10st 3lb. Johnny Bradburne, the 'old' amateur, discusses prospects with Andy Orkney who rides the grey Howe Street. John White, another with a good record, sits on his own taking it all in, outwardly unfussed by it all. John Durkan, thirsty from the sauna, only found out his mount Royle Speedmaster would run the day before and has struggled with the weight.

The jockeys are called out for the first race, outside it is beginning to drizzle. There are mixed feelings about riding in an earlier race. Some, like Richard, prefer to get warmed up, others with a good ride in the big race don't want to risk their good health, they'll put it on the line in the National but what a shame to get this far and then do a collar bone an hour before. It happened to Eamon Murphy in 1986. The National used to be the third race but now it is the fourth.

Jimmy Frost, without a National ride this year, wins the first on Spinning. It is a popular success. Jimmy had been in the hotel sauna the night before. He'd prefer not to have a ride in the National now unless it's a good one. He doesn't want the memory of Little Polveir to be diminished by subsequent falls. Outside umbrellas are up and it is cold.

Mark Dwyer wins the second on Boutzdaroff but these races are peripheral to the National, side attractions, mere cake stalls at the dog show, to get the crowd warmed up. Most of the National jockeys are changed, many ready with their correct weights, ready to pass the scales when the jockeys have gone out for the next. Leathers are checked for any weakness, valets aware of the extra stress those steep drops will place upon them.

Richard and six other jockeys leave the changing room for the Martell Hurdle, the Champion re-run with Granville Again, Morley Street, Flown and four others. Over two and a half miles it is more Flown's trip. They place their goggles in their breeches or under their colours to protect them from the spitting rain, it is important to keep a clean windscreen. It is actually one hell of a race. Flown leads turning into the straight with Graham Bradley having bided his time moving into a position on Morley Street and Granville Again ready to pounce. Brad is cantering on the enigmatic Morley Street, holding on to him for as long as he dare, wanting to win only by a head. Richard cannot believe what he can see out of the corner of his eye. Morley Street has never travelled as well as he does at Flown's girth and the temptation is to slip his bridle off over his head and then see how Brad fares. But Scu, off the bridle from the third last, has switched to his outer and halfway up the run in Brad has to shake the reins at his mount, who draws away to win by one and a half lengths. Inside the changing room Brad's cool handling of the situation on Morley Street has defused much of the nervous tension and for a couple of minutes that, rather than the National, is the talking point. Even the beaten jockeys, Richard included, are agasp at Brad's performance. They are given a kick to have been witnesses to such a ride.

Barely has Richard had time to change and jockeys for the 1993 Martell Grand National are called out. It is plenty early enough everyone agrees. Some horses are still being saddled and with most of the jockeys doing light, with a minimum of clothing on, just a body protector, silks and light breeches, it is odds on they'll get cold. But, sure, it takes a while to sort out thirty-nine horses into numerical order, parade and all have girths checked at the start.

I had passed my saddle for Travel Over to Richard Lee straight after the Aintree Hurdle. The light girth had been too short and he returned for a longer one. Normally that would not present any difficulties as far as time is concerned but most other jockeys were on board when Travel Over arrived in the paddock.

The paddock before the National is usually very crowded. The weather is probably more talked about than tactics at this stage, which will have been discussed in detail earlier on. Richard's were pretty simple, to do his own thing. He knows the horse, he knows the course and the race. Instead he joked with Robert Waley-Cohen, Won't Be Gone Long's owner, and Nicky Henderson, both more suitably attired for the damp day. It is also with some pride that you parade. It is like being presented to royalty before a big football match, people who've backed you in the crowd wishing you luck. 'Go on number twenty-four, come on Richard. Our money's on you.' You become aware that millions around the world are watching live.

Out of the paddock, along a path past the hospitality area, head on towards a BBC camera, round past the stables, out on to the course. The excitement, the nerves to a large extent disappear once you are on your horse. Now it is just the pair of you with a job to do. No worries from owners or trainers.

We form two circling groups outside on the course, numbers 1 to 20 on the left, 21 to 40 on the right, sorting ourselves out into numerical order with Rodger Farrant, clerk of the course at Chepstow, organizing. We parade in front of the stands, turn and canter down to the first, have a good look at it and return to the start. Girths and breastplates are checked and when they've finished we still have another eight minutes to wait. There is a lot of camaraderie. Many of the jockeys wish each other luck, joke about the cold. 'Be lucky,' says Neale Doughty. 'Good luck Woody,' says Simon McNeill in Bonanza Boy's pink colours. Some of the jockeys call their horses' lads over to lead them round or throw a rug over their backsides. Horses are like any athletes, better warmed up and the canter to the start has now worn off. It is a long wait, like eternity. The crowd behind the starter are abusive and noisy, they sound local, most don't know what they are talking about. 'Go on Gee,' they shouted at me in genuine belief that I was my sister.

It is a relief when Captain Keith Brown, about to start his last National, calls us into line. Richard and myself are towards the outside, there are maybe only half a dozen outside of us. I want to go where I went on Mr Frisk. The main group is bunched on the innner just under the rostrum. The white tape sags in the middle under the weight of rain that has been falling on and off since lunchtime. It stretches 65 yards across the course though the outside half is almost redundant. A couple of horses are reluctant to come in, Royle Speedmaster backs away, Chatam won't come forward, Roc de Prince stands in perfect line but faces the wrong way. The starter is keen to let us go. There is some confusion though. We can see police horses cantering across the course down by the first. The starter hasn't seen them and it is only the protestations of those who can see what's happening down the track that alerts him. There are demonstrators in the way. The runners on the inside are unable to see the obstruction as they are on a bend. There is therefore some reluctance on their part to back away and lose their pole positions.

Eventually, eight minutes later the course is cleared and we are called in again. Have you ever been in the line up of the Grand National? Have you ever read Enid Bagnold's *National Velvet*? That's what it was like, surely no description of ours could match hers as The Piebald lined up. To misquote numerically: 'At the Post the thirty-nine horses were swaying like the sea. Forward . . . No good! Back again. Forward . . . No good! Back again.

'The line formed . . . and rebroke. Waves of the sea. Drawing a breath . . . breaking. Velvet fifth from the rail, between the bay and the brown. The starter had long finished his instructions. Nothing more was said aloud, but low oaths flew, the cursing and grumbling flashed like a storm. An eye glanced at her with a look of hate. The breaking of movement was too close to movement to be borne. It was like water clinging to the tilted rim of the glass, like the sound of the dreaded explosion after the great shell had fallen. The will to surge forward overlaid by something delicate and terrible and strong, human obedience at bursting point, but not broken.'

Again the same horses were reluctant to line up. Kenny Johnson is twice told to get his mount Stay On Tracks' head off the tape. We all look for a flyer, trying to anticipate the starter. 'You all right?' he shouts. That's the signal, we surge forward, the tape is broken by New Mill House and Direct. 'False start, false start,' screams Keith Brown as the field streams down towards the first. Most are aware of the situation. Richard shouts, we all shout in the confusion to those around us, 'It's a false start, pull up.' Most of us, relieved to have got going, let our horses canter to the first, have another look, one last reminder, after all it was twenty minutes ago when they last saw it. Richard tries to get Won't Be Gone Long to tread on the orange ground rail, something solid, something to respect. Some swing on to the Mildmay Course.

It takes a while for the tape to be repaired. Again we are called in, again Chatam and Royle Speedmaster are reluctant to come forward. The starter asks us to move back off the tape which should spring up and away from the horses' heads when released. The line is pretty good this time though we are close to the tape, human obedience again at bursting point. 'Come on, come on,' he shouts and the tape goes up. The inside get a clean start but on the outside Formula One, next to Won't Be Gone Long, has his nose over the tape and it doesn't spring properly. In the surge forward it snags round Richard's neck as he tries to duck under it. It is also hooked round Travel Over's front legs but the inside, the majority thinking it is a clean start, are away, oblivious to the starter's calls of false start, his voice carried away in the wind and drowned by the crowd.

The majority never saw the advance flagman, Ken Evans. Richard saw him both times and on neither occasion was his red flag raised when he approached. The second time he appeared to be legging it to safety out of the way of the charging field. Who can blame him? Keith Brown's own flag failed to unfurl and his repeated shouts of false start go unheard. Like trying to stop a pack of foxhounds after a fox, there was to be no stopping the thirty that got a clean break. The nine that remained included Richard, the tape now ensnared round his neck and being pulled tighter with every stride Travel Over took. They were still progressing towards the first but hampered by tape and Richard swerving and screaming 'false start' though he wasn't entirely sure if it had been. He was hoping.

It is a terrible feeling being left at the start in the National, like being left on a desert island by a passing ship and there was clearly going to be no stopping the others. Richard is gutted, no ride in the John Hughes and now no ride in the National. Having pulled up, he and his eight colleagues return to the start, Richard having collected the broken tape but as unsure as the punters at home watching television what is happening, the commentary continuing as if it were a normal race though John Hanmer clearly says, 'I don't know why they're continuing, it's a void race.'

On Travel Over, freed of the tape but some way behind, I set off in vain pursuit. In the confusion how was I to know whether or not the race would be declared valid at the stewards' enquiry which would surely follow? However, he was lame on landing over the first and I pulled him up, hopped off and walked back, the crowd swarming round to see if I knew what was happening. I knew less than anyone for I was not with the pack nor back at the start, I was leading my horse across the Melling Road, a furlong from the start, when they came past setting out for the second circuit, Andy Orkney on the grey Howe Street leading the way egged on by Seamus O'Neill on Sure Metal, both with their heads down like a pair of pied pipers. Most of the fancied runners had pulled up after a circuit though, Captain Dibble, Party Politics, Zeta's Lad and Garrison Savannah, Martin Pipe running on to the course to stop his runners. However, those who kept going believed those officials who were trying to stop the race were protesters.

Richard meanwhile has hopped off Won't Be Gone Long. The scene is one of complete confusion. Would they rerun the race with nine runners, would they rerun the race the next week, next season? What was happening, why couldn't they stop the field at the Chair? No-one knew. Confusion reigned. As the remaining runners returned back home from the Canal Turn, still thinking the race was on, Richard walked down in front of the stands to watch the closing stages on the giant screen. Up the run-in John White was timing a perfect run on Esha Ness, behind him the crowd booed. Never had scenes like this been seen before at Aintree. And not until he crossed the line did John realize it was a void race.

Owners, trainers and jockeys gathered around the start, some horses fresh ready to go, others tired, sweating, after completing four and a half miles. Some tempers rose; John Upson, trainer of Zeta's Lad, told the starter he would see him in court. Keith

Brown was himself given police protection that is usually reserved for the winning horse and rider. The stewards convened, reconvened, panicked. Confusion still reigned.

It was not for some time that a rerun was discounted and Won't Be Gone Long and his eight fellow non-starters could be led back to the stables, unexercised. Robert Waley-Cohen offered Richard his green trench coat and he exchanged stories with Simon McNeill and Scu. 'What will Jonathon Lower think when I jock him off Chatam for the rerun?' asked Scu with a smile remembering Cheltenham and noticing that Chatam was one of the nine that had remained at the start. Simon, like the cat that got the cream, described the ride he had had until Bonanza Boy had refused after one and a half circuits. Everyone had their own version of events, what had happened to them. It was, they agreed, a combination of many small things. Indeed this was borne out in the Jockey Club's official enquiry published just before Royal Ascot in June. Richard attended the immediate post-race enquiry, just to tell them what had happened to him. The advance flagman Ken Evans was also in there but it was obvious that a more detailed enquiry would have to be instigated.

Normally after a National one jockey gets all the glory, thirty-nine ponder what might have been or next year. This time everyone got a slice of the action and ironically the only loser was the winner, John White. Richard showered, changed and drove home, by now a dark and very wet April evening. The rain rattled the windows of the Farm House Restaurant near Frilford where Richard, Carl Llewellyn, Simon McNeill and myself met a group of friends for supper, Martin Bosley, Luke Harvey and Willie MacFarlane who had all been at Hereford. It was, we agreed, one of the most talkative evenings we have ever had.

CHAPTER TEN

APRIL

THE EXCITEMENT OF BEING part of the void Grand National was short
lived and restricted to a morning of hilarity watching a video recording
of the previous day's events. Apart from the initial disappointment
of not having a go at Aintree's challenge, Richard would have been
most unlikely to have won the race. Won't Be Gone Long had not
after all had the ideal preparation. He had missed his prep race, had
fallen schooling and, a fortnight later on, was to finish a long way
behind in the Scottish National.

However, Richard had said to anyone who had cared to ask that
he would not seriously wind himself up for the championship until
Cheltenham and Liverpool were over. Now on the Monday following
the race, with newspapers bandying about the words 'disaster',
'tragedy' and 'disgrace', there came to the wannabe-champion's
attention a rumour, from neighbour and colleague Graham Bradley,
that Peter Scudamore was on the brink of retirement. Richard
had rung his agent, Robert Kington, whose sister Marilyn was

married to Scu, to see whether the story was true. Scu had never intimated to Richard any desire to hang up his boots and Robert was quick to refute the suggestions.

There is no racing in the south on the Monday and Tuesday following the National and while the national debate about the fiasco raged, Richard was psyching himself up for the remaining two months of the season. They were going to be the hardest two months with Scu breathing down his neck. Traditionally it has been a strong time for Martin Pipe's yard and Richard's lead of fifteen was a cushion but nothing a hungry and determined Scu couldn't peg back with Pipe behind him. At the same time Richard was continuing to have treatment on his hand which remained a constant source of aggravation.

'The first I knew about it was at 8.30 a.m. when a reporter from BBC Ceefax rang up to ask me for a comment. "A comment about what?" I asked. A comment about Scu's retirement,' recalls Richard. 'Without a doubt it was the most shocked I have ever been. I was genuinely shocked. I had spent the last two days preparing myself for probably the hardest two months mentally of my whole career. The pressure was immense. I was revved up, ready to give it a kick. Of course, after it had sunk in there was huge relief, a release. I knew I'd be able to enjoy the last couple of months of the season. Adrian Maguire was thirty-nine behind, but as long as I kept on riding winners and remained in more or less one piece it meant the championship was just about mine. But words cannot express the admiration I had for Scu. We will miss him very much in the weighing room.' Scu, then contracted to write for the *Daily Telegraph*, had announced to the world his retirement in the newspaper. It is always sad when a top sportsman retires, though heaven knows, how much better a month too early than a month too late.

It is something that had clearly been playing on Scu's mind lately as he had pointed out in his valedictory article. There was obviously going to be a big crowd at Ascot and whatever else it did, it was going to take a certain amount of pressure off the National incident which was still headlining.

Scu was to have three rides on his last day, Grand Hawk in the first, Dagobertin in the fourth and the last ride of his career on Sweet Duke for his great friend and neighbour Nigel Twiston-Davies in the

Alpine Meadow Handicap Hurdle. Richard won the first on Hebridean, the horse that Carol had ridden at York seemingly so long ago last summer. It was a wet, wintery day and the hurdle course at Ascot was heavy.

Scu bowed out as you'd have expected with a winner, Sweet Duke doing the honours and running out the four-length winner, the 1,678th of a fifteen-year career. Scu had been an exemplary champion in every respect, on and off the pitch, a gentleman and ambassador for the sport.

However, his retirement left open the question of who would be his successor as first jockey to Martin Pipe's West Country yard. On the face of it there are three contenders, Richard himself, Irish Champion Charlie Swan and the younger talent, the man they call the champion-in-waiting, Adrian Maguire, who had first been brought to the British racing public's attention when riding Omerta to victory for Pipe in the Kim Muir at Cheltenham.

Richard has a chat to Scu during his final afternoon. What is the best plan of attack? They discuss several things about the job which puts Richard in an even bigger quandary. Martin Pipe had helped make Scu champion for the last six of his eight championships. Though there was a general assumption Pipe was a quantity and not quality man he had some very good horses in his yard, he had the Champion hurdler Granville Again, Chatam, Run For Free, Lord Relic and Carvill's Hill. It would be an exciting new challenge, new faces all round, but against that he pays no retainer.

The Duke also has some very promising horses for the following season, Viking Flagship, Carobee would be back, Wonder Man, Baydon Star and old favourites like Another Coral and Waterloo Boy. He was also expanding and would have more horses. However he wanted a definite first claim on Richard, not the uncertainty of having Richard decide between Jackdaw's Castle's horses and Nicky Henderson's. Nicky, too, wanted first claim. It was clearly going to be hard to tie the two jobs up again without upsetting both parties.

At one stage in the proceeding, the Duke appeared happy with the situation and Nicky was coming round, as long as he had first claim on Richard for a couple of the best horses he did not mind. However the Duke did not want to be left in the cold. He needed to know Richard's plans. A suitable alternative might be snapped up by someone else if he was not careful so he kept in touch with Richard, letting him know what he was doing about it and setting time limits on any decision. Richard meanwhile had meetings with Martin Pipe who first of all wanted to discuss any appointment with his owners and wanted to have a good look at the other two contenders, Adrian and Charlie.

Things came to a head on 3 May when the Duke announced that Adrian Maguire would be his stable jockey for the 1993/94 season. Richard finalized the job with Martin Pipe the following day at Newton Abbot where he rode a double for him. Scu had retired on 7 April and it had taken less than a month for the major changes in the jockey-go-round to slot into place.

'It was very hard', recalls Richard, 'to desert all those decent horses with the Duke and a decent retainer. We had seven great years together; and on the whole a superb working relationship. But had Scu pushed he could have been champion this season. Whoever takes the job has a favourite's chance of being champion and it presents a fresh challenge, fresh horses.'

In the meantime April had ticked on. The season slackens off enabling busy jockeys a chance to catch their breath though evening meetings from the middle of the month onwards can mean long days and hair-raising dashes from one meeting to another through rush-hour traffic. The week following the National was quiet after Scu's retirement with little jump racing until Easter Saturday. On Good Friday it rained cats and dogs which was unfortunate for the organizers of Lambourn's annual open day and the demonstration schooling session on the Mandown.

Easter Monday is the traditional date for the Irish National run at Fairyhouse. In 1990 it had provided Richard with one of his greatest thrills when Desert Orchid won. Now he had an equally good chance of repeating that success on Rushing Wild, the Gold Cup second. Only a week before Richard had been deliberating. 'Do I ride Rushing Wild in Ireland or do I stay at home and try to ride a winner in the quest for the Championship?' He chose the former although Scu's retirement had meant that the latter was an almost foregone conclusion.

Richard is as at home riding in Ireland as he is at Newbury or Ascot. If anything it gives him more pleasure. Rushing Wild has a serious chance in the Irish National. Favourite for the race was Zeta's Lad, John Upson's gelding who had completed a circuit of the void National nine days earlier. Rushing Wild, one of the other four British challengers that also included Royal Athlete, Sibton Abbey and Cool Ground who had all finished behind him in the Gold Cup, was top-weight with 12 st. Upson's comments on television in the heat of the moment following the National had been misconstrued by some of the Irish, his life and horses had been threatened. However relations between Ireland and Upson had since been repaired.

Rushing Wild and Richard made most of the running, jumping for fun, gaining a length in the air at most obstacles but approaching the sixteenth off a bend he changed legs and suddenly went very lame behind. He had fractured his pelvis, a wonderful career cut tragically short as he was humanely destroyed. What a leveller this sport can be. Ebony Jane, a horse whom Richard had been second on twice and whom he had been asked to ride by Francis Flood, went on to win the race under Charlie Swan.

At Cheltenham, the last meeting of the season under Cleeve Hill for professionals proved a lucky meeting for Richard, not so for Jimmy Frost. Le Piccolage won the Golden Miller Handicap beating the former Gold Cup winner Cool Ground eight lengths. It was his first run since finishing second to Zeta's Lad at Christmas. In this race, though, David Barons' runner, Roctor, dropped his hindlegs in the open ditch, a typical example of the Cheltenham ditch fall that we talked about before the Festival. Jimmy suffered concussion which meant a mandatory week on the sidelines recuperating. Immediately he would miss the ride in the next race but one, on Beech Road, but more seriously he would miss the ride on Topsham Bay, winner of the race a year earlier, in the Whitbread Gold Cup at Sandown in three days' time.

Richard came in for both spare rides. As soon as David Barons knew Jimmy would be unfit to ride he approached Richard, without a ride in the big race. He is only too pleased to accept and celebrates by making all the running on Beech Road to win by threequarters of a length.

Whitbread day at Sandown is always special. It is now about the only meeting where flat racing shares the card with jumping and besides the Whitbread is the Threshers Classic Trial for potential Derby horses. In Ireland most meetings are mixed out of necessity but here the two codes are kept apart sadly. There is always a big crowd, it is always attended by the Queen Mother who has won the race in the past with Special Cargo, and all the best flat jockeys are present. Topsham Bay's weight of 10st is a struggle for Richard, especially now as the season is beginning to draw out and racing is less regular.

Topsham Bay is a big horse but a wonderful, agile ride. Richard, 1lb overweight despite protestations from John McCririck on Channel Four, has him handy all the way. There are few such wonderful sights as a bunching Whitbread field coming to the Pond fence, the third last, all jostling for position. Givus A Buck had been in the rear early on but had made steady progress to lead at the seventeenth fence and from there on was never really headed. Topsham Bay put in an almighty leap at the second last to keep himself in contention with the leader and another good jump at the last helped. Paul Holley and Givus A Buck drifted right up the steep Sandown hill bumping Topsham Bay, knocking him off his stride. In a rousing finish Givus A Buck won by a head but he had clearly transgressed the rules. A stewards' enquiry was announced soon after they pulled up.

It is amazing how often horses do drift across on that hill. Only twelve months earlier Topsham Bay had done the same thing though he had been far enough clear for it to have made no difference to any other runner. What is more, in the history of the race there had been two dubious stewards' decisions. Firstly, Proud Tarquin had been disqualified in 1974 and the race awarded to The Dikler. It is a decision that annoys Proud Tarquin's rider John Oaksey to this day. Secondly, and more recently, Cahervillahow and Charlie Swan had been disqualified in favour of Docklands Express in 1991. Many thought that if they had had the races taken off them then surely Givus A Buck would lose this one. Of the three cases this must be the clearest cut of interference that there had been.

Stewards' enquiries are formal affairs. There's little room for humour though for John Francome in the old days they had been a stage for some of his best pranks. On one occasion all the jockeys in one race had been summoned in for not wanting to line up. John had stood behind Steve Smith-Eccles who had his hands cupped behind his back. Seizing the opportunity John took something out of his breeches (bearing in mind there are no pockets) and put it in Eccy's hands. When Eccy realized what he was feeling he jumped a mile. Another time, John was called in so often that the final time he went in he took his own chair with him.

Both jockeys are called for at the same time and, standing in front of a table, are introduced to each steward and the stewards' secretary (stipe), who guides the local stewards as to the relevant rules and whether or not they have been breached. Each jockey puts his case forward. You don't have to swear on the bible and winning races in the stewards' room is something of an art in a marginal case.

Parties then watch any video evidence there might be, head on angles, side on and occasionally from behind. The stewards ask any questions and the jockeys have a final chance to make any points they consider relevant before being asked to leave the room while the stewards, again guided by the stipe, make a decision.

Richard, on this occasion, was rushing off to Worcester. The timing was tight without this hold up and he was worried that if he did get the race then the presentation would prevent him from reaching Worcester in time to partner Master Jolson. Before the result was announced he was asked to put his colours back on in case and as he returned with Paul Holley into the stewards' room to hear the outcome he caught the tannoy announcing the amended result. He knew that he had won. Outside, protocol was broken so that Richard could rush off to Worcester and instead of being presented with his trophy last, a golden hind's head (the Whitbread logo), the Queen Mother made his presentation before owner Sir Eric Parker and trainer David Barons. The trip to Worcester by car took an hour and forty minutes where Master Jolson finished second.

Though at this time Richard could relax in the knowledge that the championship was assured, speculation about which job he would have for next season travelled with him to Punchestown for their Festival the following week. Punchestown is about threequarters of an hour from Dublin. Ciaran O'Toole had told Richard someone would pick him up from the airport and sure enough they did. Two off-duty gardai (policemen) whose hobby was racing met him. Their squad car had been recently rammed and they were reduced to driving a small Ford Fiesta. Nevertheless, outside the airport out came a magnetic blue light which was placed on the roof, switched on and they sped unhindered through the worst of the Dublin traffic. It was the best lift Richard had ever had to the races.

Unlike Cheltenham and Aintree, Punchestown, a festival of racing reaping the rewards of the Irish Tourist Board's enterprise, is a successful meeting for Richard. It is picturesque and has a relaxed atmosphere about it. It is well attended by British racegoers. The course, five miles from Naas but otherwise in the middle of nowhere, is very nearly two miles round and for a two-mile race you start with your backs to the last. His first ride is on Bayrouge, a half-sister to the infamous Duntree, trained by Ann-Marie Crowley-O'Brien. A tough good stamp of a five-year-old she had already won eight times during the season. She had shown no worthwhile form at home of late, though, and Joe Crowley had told Richard she was just as likely to finish last as first. In the paddock despite having run many races this season she looks well but on the larger side. During the Country Pride Champion Novices' Hurdle she is always near the front and always travelling well, jumping quickly. She takes it up at the third last, and despite Richard's worries that he might be in front too soon, she keeps on well to win by four lengths. A fine start.

In the next, the BMW Drogheda Handicap Chase, Viking Flagship, brought over by the Duke after missing Cheltenham and Liverpool on the fast ground, enjoys the going which is just on the soft side of good. He had won his previous four races and but for falling first time out would have been unbeaten. Killiney Graduate sets a blistering pace but Viking Flagship, who had pitched on his nose at the first ditch past the stands, has him covered and when he makes a mistake at the fourth last Richard takes up the running. At the second last Kevin Morgan drives Foulksrath Castle up Richard's inner and looks momentarily like threatening but a superb leap at the last seals it for Viking Flagship who wins by two and a half lengths.

In the last Nicky Henderson's Thinking Twice, a maiden over hurdles, wins the Berkeley Court Handicap Hurdle. Owned by the Million In Mind partnership headed by David Minton who buys many of Nicky's horses, Thinking Twice arrives at the front at the second last and it is just a question of holding on, which he does with a length to spare. Winning at Punchestown does not quite carry the clout of winning at Cheltenham but it is not far off it and who knows, maybe in a couple of years as the meeting grows it will equal it.

The evenings are spent at Benny and Sheila Powell's beautiful Swordstown Stud, within walking distance of the course. The Duke is also staying there as are Brendan Powell, Richard's colleague and the Powell's son and his fiancée Rachel. After supper they drive into

Naas for a drink and it seems most of the racegoers have returned
to the town for their evening's entertainment.

The second day, the last Wednesday in April, begins with a pile up
in the Naas Traders' Mares' Hurdle Final. Richard rides Sylvia Fox,
the favourite in the two-and-a-half-mile race. There are twenty-one
runners and Charlie Swan, leading jockey at Cheltenham with four
winners, is up near the front but it is a rough race with much
scrimmaging. At one point he is squeezed against the rails. He
bounces off them and his mount falls bringing down three or four
behind him. Richard, also on the inner, is relieved that the mêlée
leaves a narrow gap for him along the rails. It is a sickening sight to
be passing horses falling like ninepins with the horrible sound effects
of clicking heels and the wind being knocked out of half a ton of
horseflesh. 'I really thought they'd be digging Charlie out,' recalls
Richard. 'It was stomach churning to hear the cries of jockeys as
they went down unable to steer round it.'

There are dolls across the course where the pile up took place
near the second last and when the field come round for the last time
a jockey and horse are still on the ground but, unbelievably and to
everyone's relief, none of the jockeys are seriously hurt, although
a horse is put down. Charlie even goes on to win the next race.
The rest of the day is less exciting. Strong Beau runs as if slightly
over the top, Graham Bradley wins on Fissure Seal which will put
him in good form for the evening when he, too, is staying with the
Powells. British trainer Bryan Smart had wanted Richard to ride his
runner Carrickrovaddy in the three-mile chase at 10lb overweight and
Richard had refused, accepting instead a ride in the race for Eddie
Harty which pulled up. Carrickrovaddy finished towards the rear but
Richard still comes in for some grief from his owners.

Thursday begins with a double for Charlie and is followed by
another victory for Brad on Bishops Hall. In this race Richard is
second on Second Schedual for Arthur Moore but again it is not
without incident. Tom Taaffe, Arthur's stable jockey, rides the stable's other runner in the race, New Mill House. Tom is upsides in
front going towards the third last with a position on the middle-inner
when he sees Brendan Sheriden trying to push up his inside. Sharp
as you like he takes Brendan onto the hurdle track trying to force
him wide of the fence wing. Ironically it is New Mill House who,

finding himself perilously close to the wing of the fence, ducks out. Brendan swerved back in clipping his foot on the wing and managed to jump the fence although it cost him any chance he had of winning. This incident had unwittingly left Richard in front too soon, just what he didn't want over this extended three miles, a trip a quarter of a mile beyond Second Schedual's optimum. The stewards' enquiry into Tom's misbehaviour lasts most of the rest of the day, with Richard acting as a witness for the defence. 'Having seen the film the defence was limited,' says Richard. Tom was stood down for fourteen days.

It was always the intention to run Viking Flagship twice in three days if he came out of his first race well. He is a stuffy, tough horse and after the Duke had seen him the first night he thought he'd be able to run in the Bank of Ireland Novices' Chase, again over two miles. This time he was up against Soft Day, the best novice in Ireland, How's the Boss and Antonin, another English raider, whom he had beaten fifteen lengths at level weights earlier in the season. However Antonin had shown a marked improvement since. He makes all the running and when he jumps to the left at the second last Richard switches Viking Flagship to the inner and cruises into the front. Despite jumping left himself at the last, he still runs out a comfortable four-length winner. On returning to scale, Richard can see Arthur Moore looking shatterered. His Soft Day, whose challenge had never materialized, had in fact broken a leg and had been put down, a sad loss to Irish racing.

Richard rounds off the meeting with a second on Duhallow Lodge for Willie Mullins in the three-mile handicap hurdle. He is told to be handy and that the horse stays the distance well. After a ragged start Duhallow Lodge pulls his way to the front in what is a slow-run race. At the second he has no semblance of control, he's tried fighting the horse now he chucks the reins at it. If a horse has nothing to pull against it often drops the bridle. It remains in front but is collared at the last. The meeting had ended well, four winners from twelve rides in three days and the journey back to Dublin is less hectic than it was coming out.

MAY

The season now begins to slacken off and wind down. There are a few hectic days yet, rushing from a day meeting to a night one but nothing to the pressure Richard had assumed he would be under. One Friday he drove from Newton Abbot to Bangor, a three and a half hour journey shared with Carl Llewellyn. Thinking Twice won again at Haydock, he rode a three-timer at Chepstow then added another at Towcester that evening. Many of his twenty-two winners, his most productive May, were supplied by Martin Pipe which was helping cement their new relationship. At Perth he rode the Duke's 100th winner of the season, his first century, a remarkable feat considering it was his first exploratory year at Jackdaw's Castle, and Nicky Henderson's last three runners all won. There are even days now when he can sit outside Hyperion House relaxing in the sun before going evening racing, recharging the batteries.

JUNE

The first Saturday in June. On the whole it has been a wet spring, indeed there's been nothing about the weather to suggest it is even early summer. Only a couple of weeks ago Lambourn was all but washed away in a thunderstorm; Faringdon, a small town north of Hyperion House, was. Now a layer of mist hugs the hayfields in the mornings on the way to ride out, like a ghostly shroud, the grass heavy with dew, sunlight pierces the curtains before even jockeys wish to be woken. Surely this is the season of mists, not autumn – did Keats never venture out before breakfast?

Today, 5 June, is one of the first days you could really say is summer. The sun glares through puffy cotton-wool clouds; the trumpet-shaped flowers of the foxglove buzz with insect life, and husbands in shorts, beer in hand, decide the time is right to clean up the barbecue set. Along wooded lanes the smell of elderflower is overpowering, in gardens catmint and lavender scent the air.

In sport it's been one of those weeks. At Old Trafford the first test in the 1993 Ashes series is delicately poised; on a slow wet wicket the previously unknown spinners have it. At Woburn Peter Baker leads the Dunhill British Masters Golf tournament; Nick Faldo, undisputedly the sport's best last year, has twice hit the ball out of bounds. At Epsom the best staying fillies line up three days after Commander in Chief, a second string for Henry Cecil, has run away with flat racing's Blue Riband to beat two 150–1 shots for second and third respectively. Even the fourth was 50–1 and Tenby, given the 'wonderhorse' tag of the odds-on shot, trails in tenth, his name consigned to the backburner. That very same evening there was defeat for the leaden-legged England soccer team, made to look like a village side against little Norway. There's a pile up in the Milk Race and Steffi Graf loses the first set in the finals of the French Championships at Roland Garros in Paris. How unpredictable sport can be.

Stratford-upon-Avon is an unlikely stage to wind up our story, well not entirely Stratford. Richard has a further two rides at Market Rasen in the evening. Our nature suggests we ought go no further than the afternoon meeting with most of the other jockeys. There's a limit to our dedication and it's probably why the majority of us will never be champions. There's no limit to Richard's dedication. We're nearly a season on from where we started and he's still willing to learn, still willing to make the two-hour journey on to Market Rasen. This is one job where even the champions admit you can never achieve absolute perfection but this one is still willing to learn, still pushing himself to achieve the impossible even now in the last mile of the marathon, the last battle in the war, the last round in the ring, on the last day of the season.

The drive to Stratford is a familiar one. In the 'old days' (a couple of years ago) we used to go through Stow-on-the-Wold, Moreton-in-Marsh, across Warwickshire. A twisty trip, in the winter you'd often drive past hunting hounds, in the summer you queued to get into Stratford behind caravans, American tourists in search of Anne Hathaway's cottage or the theatre, in search of their fix of history. Now it is Oxford, M40, Stratford. Easy as pie but not so interesting. The M40 is our most travelled motorway now, how did we manage without it? The landmarks are familiar: the sweet smell that drifts across the road from a chocolate factory near Banbury; the old air-raid shelters overgrown with brambles on an old aerodrome now bisected by six lanes of concrete and tarmac; fields of runner beans; the fading yellow of rape; past open-top cars. A glider hangs over Stratford and swoops away over the horizon on an invisible thermal, you pass the turn for Hampton Lucy and think to yourself what a pretty village it must be if the name is any indication. You pass white lilac, now like the barbecue set turning rust-coloured, its season ending too. Next to it a maytree in full pink. The traffic policeman, in shirt sleeves, directs you into the course where they expect their biggest crowd of the season and can guarantee a better atmosphere than there was at Epsom on Wednesday.

Richard Dunwoody walks to the changing room with the same eager enthusiasm as he did for day one of this season. He answers a summery-looking punter's question, 'Know anything, Richard?' like a politician. 'Beech Road should go all right in the first.' It is like saying the grass is green. We all know Beech Road should run all right, he'll be odds on and anyway, even if he's second, that'll come into the vague category of 'all right'. But, for all Richard knows the unknown punter may be the man who barracked him at Wolverhampton in March. He signs an autograph for a little boy, perhaps an aspiring Dunwoody who will ride races one day. Shows his medical book, greets John and Tom Buckingham, his valets, for the last time until August. He looks like he doesn't want the season to end. There's an end-of-term atmosphere in all but Richard's corner.

A few final touches have been applied for next season. The last piece of the jockey merry-go-round that he created by accepting the Martin Pipe job has fitted into place. Mick Fitzgerald, an up-and-coming young rider, will share the rides with Richard at Nicky Henderson's Seven Barrows. Adrian Maguire, of course, will be riding for David Nicholson and the Jackdaw's Castle team. Perhaps, it is the end of that era that Richard regrets, not the last day of the season. He slips a towel round his waist and heads for the sauna. A last pound to drip onto the slatted floor.

He dries himself off, hoists nylon tights round his hips, his face drawn and flushed by the 10st 1lb he is attempting, next breeches then boots. The only good thing about riding in the heat is that you can lose a pound or pound and a half in each race as opposed to half a pound in winter. His suit is neatly folded into his bag, ready for the dash to Market Rasen.

The champion doesn't ride a winner on the last day, how unpredictable sport can be. Beech Road, former champion hurdler himself, at one stage shares a twenty-length lead. Jumps the last in front. This, in a week of sporting upsets, is not going to be another, you can rely on Dunwoody as he gets down behind Beech Road's neck to drive him out. Initially, he holds Deb's Ball but in the last 100 yards that horse finds another gear and Beech Road has no response a second time. An old man in a pork-pie hat, disgruntled punter or madman or both, barracks the unsaddling jockey. 'Where were you Dunwoody? He's been twenty-five lengths behind.' The liver chestnut stands heaving in the paddock, Dunwoody doesn't hear the protestations and he returns to the weighing room for the 734th time this British season.

Inside the jockey's sanctuary he languishes against a white-washed pillar, the seams of his body protector are damp with sweat, he studies the replay, the quest for knowledge is never ending in this game. The Black Monk, for Martin Pipe, is third in the staying hurdle, Millrous third in the claiming hurdle, Bold in Combat unplaced in the three-mile handicap chase.

Outside the course, by the horse gate, his car waits purring, ready for its last journey of the season. A taxi lingers for Adrian Maguire, a champion in waiting, in order that he can catch a light plane to Market Rasen. Tired horses walk past back to the stables, sweat drips from underneath their bellies but they've recovered their breath. At this stage of the season they're all fit. Richard Dunwoody arrives at the jog, bag in hand. To his left a valet carries his three saddles. They are flung in the boot and he's already on his way.

One hour, fifty-five minutes, an egg sandwich and Lucozade bottle later, he arrives at the small Lincolnshire market town. His arrival coincides with the ending of the Fling Fling Novices' Chase. An ambulance, blue lights flashing, siren blaring, passes him on the road to the course. He knows immediately that a colleague has been hurt, badly. As a rule they take you to the racecourse medical room if it is not life-threatening or not serious. It is like being shot on the last day of the war. It doesn't matter that it's an amateur that Richard has never met nor heard of before. It is still the same sickening feeling, poor bugger, so nearly made it. On the weighing-room steps, another, Geoff Harker, has his wing up, a broken collar bone.

Tri Folene and Highland Spirit, with ten wins to her credit since it all began at Bangor forty-four weeks ago, finish third and second respectively. We'd have expected one winner from Richard's four favourites on the last day. Neither the probable nor the possible occurred. A former champion, Jonjo O'Neill, presents Richard, Mick Fitzgerald, leading conditional jockey, and Andrew Thornton, leading amateur, with a bottle of champagne each after the Seasons Over Novices' Hurdle.

Our would-be champion can now drop the prefix. Between the end of last season and the end of the 1992/93 season he has in total ridden in 824 races, 825 if you include the Race That Never Was, the 1993 Grand National. Of those 739 were in Britain where he rode 173 winners, 78 were in Ireland where he rode 15 winners, 3 were in Jersey, 2 were in America, 2 in Belgium. He hit the deck no less than 45 times.

There is a Spanish saying which, roughly translated, means, 'Luck is nothing more than very close attention to detail.' Thomas Richard Dunwoody made his own luck during the 1992/93 National Hunt season which ended like it began and continued, hell for leather.

On Saturday, 12 June 1993, Richard Dunwoody was awarded the MBE in the Queen's Birthday Honours. In his championship year it was, as he says, not only a great surprise and tremendous honour, it was the best winner he rode all season.

JULY

On Monday, 12 July 1993, Richard Dunwoody celebrated his championship with a large party at the Farm House Restaurant, Frilford, near Oxford. The music was provided by the top Irish folk band The Saw Doctors.

Full name: Thomas Richard Dunwoody

Born: 18 January 1964

Parents: George Dunwoody (former Antrim trainer) and Gillian, daughter of trainer Dick Thrale

Apprenticeship: Amateur rider with Paul Kelleway, John Bosley, Tim Forster

First win: Game Trust (Colin Nash) Cheltenham, 4 May 1983

First big-race win: Prideaux Boy (1984 Mecca Bookmakers' Handicap Hurdle)

First Grand National ride: West Tip (fell, 1985)

First win for Martin Pipe: Au Bon, Uttoxeter, 28 March 1989

Grand National winner: West Tip (1986)

Champion steeplechasers: Highland Bud (1989 Breeders' Cup Chase, Colonial Cup, 1992 Breeders' Cup Chase), **Desert Orchid** (1989 King George VI Chase, 1990 Racing Post Chase, Irish Grand National, King George VI Chase, 1991 Agfa Diamond Chase), **Remittance Man** (1991 Arkle Challenge Trophy, 1992 Arlington Premier Chase Final, Melling Chase)

Champion hurdler: Kribensis (1988 Triumph Hurdle, Gerry Feilden Hurdle, Christmas Hurdle, 1989 Christmas Hurdle, 1990 Champion Hurdle)

Cheltenham Festival winners: Von Trappe (1985 Coral Golden Hurdle Final), West Tip (1985 National Hunt Handicap Chase), French Union (1987 Grand Annual Chase), Charter Party (1988 Cheltenham Gold Cup), Kribensis (1988 Triumph Hurdle, 1990 Champion Hurdle), Waterloo Boy (1989 Arkle Challenge Trophy), Bigsun (1990 National Hunt Handicap Chase), Remittance Man (1991 Arkle Challenge Trophy), Thetford Forest (1992 Sun Alliance Hurdle), Montelado (1992 Festival Bumper), Thumbs Up (1993 County Hurdle)

Other big-race wins: West Tip (1985 Anthony Mildmay Peter Cazalet Memorial Chase), Very Promising (1986 Mackeson Gold Cup, Black & White Whisky Champion Chase), The Thinker (1986 Rowland Meyrick Chase), Charter Party (1988 Gainsborough Chase), Celtic Chief (1988 Aintree Hurdle), Mr Frisk (1989 Anthony Mildmay Peter Cazalet Memorial Chase), Grey Salute (1989 Tote Gold Trophy), Norton's Coin (1989 South Wales Showers Mira Silver Trophy), Waterloo Boy (1990, 91 Castleford Chase, 1992 Victor Chandler Chase), Aquilifer (1991 Martell Cup), Another Coral (1991 Mackeson Gold Cup 1992 Tripleprint Gold Cup), Morley Street (1992 Aintree Hurdle), Mighty Mogul (1992 Gerry Feilden Hurdle, Christmas Hurdle), Topsham Bay (1993 Whitbread Gold Cup)

Champion jump jockey (races won): 1992/93

Champion jump jockey (money won): 1989/90, 1990/91, 1991/92, 1992/93

Jump Jockey of the Year: Derby Award 1991, Lester Award 1992

Five wins in a day: Chepstow, 7 November 1992

Number of centuries: 4

Most wins in a British season: 173 in 1992/93

Main stables: David Nicholson 1986-93, Martin Pipe from 1993

DUNWOODY'S CAREER TOTALS

Season	Wins	Season	Wins
1982/83	4	1988/89	91
1983/84	24	1989/90	102
1984/85	46	1990/91	127
1985/86	55	1991/92	137
1986/87	70	1992/93	173 *
1987/88	79	**TOTAL**	**908**

denotes champion jockey (races won)

© Racing Post

1992 – 93 SEASON: TOP TEN

JOCKEY AND LOWEST RIDING WEIGHT SINCE JUNE 92	TRAINER GIVING MOST WINNERS	WINS-RIDES	ALL RIDES 2ND	3RD	£1 STAKE	WIN & PLACE £ PRIZE MONEY	HURDLES WINS-RIDES	CHASES WINS-RIDES	FAVOURITES WINS-RIDES	LAST 14 DAYS WINS-RIDES	RIDES SINCE WIN	WINS-RIDES
R Dunwoody 10-0	D Nicholson	74-193 38%	121	89	-97.22	1,101,876	88-424	85-316	108-251	3-23	11	173-740 23%
P Scudamore 10-0	M C Pipe	105-325 32%	75	47	-14.91	855,603	88-272	41-144	95-211	0-0	0	129-416 31%
A Maguire 9-10	G B Balding	18-110 16%	117	97	-25.97	678,284	63-424	62-298	53-137	3-24	5	125-722 17%
P Niven 10-2	Mrs M Reveley	62-180 34%	62	52	+42.82	406,066	64-246	44-139	69-134	3-5	2	108-385 28%
J Osborne 10-0	O Sherwood	25-136 18%	71	61	+14.50	481,288	53-300	49-201	50-121	1-6	2	102-501 20%
G McCourt 10-4	N Tinkler	20-92 22%	62	61	-45.34	313,657	42-266	28-165	33-83	1-6	0	70-431 16%
N Doughty 10-7	G Richards	68-245 28%	36	33	-21.08	315,444	26-127	43-135	44-79	2-5	1	69-262 26%
C Llewellyn 10-0	N A Twiston-Davies	29-122 24%	43	49	+59.86	491,230	39-253	29-158	23-62	0-10	11	68-411 17%
M Dwyer 9-12	J G FitzGerald	33-143 23%	58	47	-86.13	461,174	31-202	30-115	37-102	2-7	0	61-317 19%
C Grant 10-0	W A Stephenson	16-87 18%	56	49	-142.62	244,930	25-225	33-194	26-65	1-8	1	58-419 14%